KRISTI YAMAGUCHI

ASIAN AMERICANS OF ACHIEVEMENT

Margaret Cho

Daniel Inouye

Michelle Kwan

Bruce Lee

Maya Lin

Yo-Yo Ma

Isamu Noguchi

Amy Tan

Vera Wang

Kristi Yamaguchi

ASIAN AMERICANS
OF ACHIEVEMENT

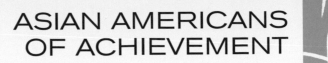

KRISTI YAMAGUCHI

JUDY L. HASDAY, EDM, COA

CHELSEA HOUSE
PUBLISHERS

An imprint of Infobase Publishing

Kristi Yamaguchi

Chelsea House
An imprint of Infobase Publishing
132 West 31st Street
New York, NY 10001

ISBN-10: 0-7910-9288-7
ISBN-13: 978-0-7910-9288-0

Library of Congress Cataloging-in-Publication Data
Hasday, Judy L., 1957–
   Kristi Yamaguchi / Judy L. Hasday.
      p. cm.—(Asian Americans of achievement)
   Includes bibliographical references and index.
   ISBN 0-7910-9288-7 (hardcover)
   1. Yamaguchi, Kristi. 2. Figure skaters United States Biography.
3. Women figure skaters United States Biography. I. Title. II. Series.
   GV850.Y36H37 2007
   796.91'2092—dc22
   [B]

2006026063

Chelsea House books are available at special discounts when purchased in bulk quantities for businesses, associations, institutions, or sales promotions. Please call our Special Sales Department in New York at (212) 967-8800 or (800) 322-8755.

You can find Chelsea House on the World Wide Web at http://www.chelseahouse.com

Text design by Erika K. Arroyo
Cover design by Ben Peterson

Printed in the United States of America
Bang NMSG 10 9 8 7 6 5 4 3 2 1

This book is printed on acid-free paper.

All links and Web addresses were checked and verified to be correct at the time of publication. Because of the dynamic nature of the Web, some addresses and links may have changed since publication and may no longer be valid.

CONTENTS

1

Always Dream

Kristi Yamaguchi was just 21 years old when she stepped onto the ice to compete for the gold medal in the women's individual figure skating competition in 1992 at the XVI Olympic Winter Games in Albertville, France. Over a 68-year span and the 16 Winter Games held during that time, 50 gold, silver, and bronze medals had been awarded. Only 4 gold medals, however, had been won by American women. Sonja Henie of Norway had been the only figure skater ever to win more than two gold, and her feat was even more incredible because she accomplished it in three Olympic Games in a row (1928, 1932, 1936).

A lifetime of training and practicing doesn't guarantee even making the U.S. Olympic Team. Thousands of little girls all across the United States have dreamed of skating in the Olympics and winning the gold medal. Very few ever make it to the top-level competitions; even fewer make it onto the Olympic team. At the close of the 1988 Winter Games in Calgary, Alberta, Canada, only 12 American women had won Olympic gold, silver, or bronze medals. The odds of making Olympic history by winning the gold medal are very slim. Despite the overwhelming odds, though, it is a dream few are willing to relinquish, even as they prepare to step on the ice in front of the judges and the crowds that pack the arena to watch the competition unfold.

A GROUP OF CHALLENGING COMPETITORS

Kristi Yamaguchi is one of those people who enters a sport radiating a special charisma. Yamaguchi always dreamed of being a professional skater and competing in the Olympics. She trained hard, sacrificed much, and gave her all to her skating. Gifted and talented, her artistry and grace on the ice had earned her a coveted spot on the 1992 U.S. Olympic women's figure skating team. Only the top three skaters in the country earn the honor of representing the United States at the Olympics. Joining Yamaguchi on the 1992 U.S. team were rivals Nancy Kerrigan and Tonya Harding. All three knew one another well and were vying to become the top women's figure skater in the United States and the world.

The competitions had been close. In 1991, Tonya Harding won the U.S. Nationals title; Yamaguchi won it in 1992, and Kerrigan won in 1993. All three women had also medaled at the World Figure Skating Championships: Yamaguchi was crowned champion in both 1991 and 1992. Harding and Kerrigan came in second and third, respectively, in 1991, and Kerrigan came in second behind Yamaguchi in 1992. Yamaguchi (1998) and Kerrigan (2004) have also both been honored by being inducted into the U.S. Figure Skating Hall of Fame, joining such distinguished past honorees as Tenley Albright, Peggy Fleming, and Dorothy Hamill.

CAPTURING GOLD

Despite the dominance of the sport in the early 1990s by U.S. women, other countries had their own great female figure skaters, too. Close rivals, and possible spoilers in America's quest for Olympic gold in Albertville, were Japan's athletic

Kristi Yamaguchi skates in the free skating portion of the women's figure skating competition at the XVI Winter Olympic Games in Albertville, France, in 1992.

sensation Midori Ito and China's five-time Nationals Champion (1990–1995), Lu Chen. Ito's ability to land some of the more difficult jumps earned her the World Figure Skating title in 1989. She was the first Asian gold medalist, and became the first woman to land the very difficult triple axel maneuver in a major international competition. Lu Chen was always in the hunt for the gold, earning a third-place finish in the Worlds in 1992, and a bronze medal in the 1994 Olympic Winter Games in Lillihammer, Norway, behind silver medalist Nancy Kerrigan.

As the Winter Games began in Albertville, Yamaguchi was the favorite for women's figure skating. Yamaguchi's skating strong points were her graceful skating and the terrific artistry and choreography she infused into her performances. Still, figure skating had become much more athletically oriented since the days of her hero Dorothy Hamill. More and more emphasis was being put on a skater's ability to execute difficult jumps, spins, and landings in their programs. Ito was the athlete and had already accomplished cleanly landing the more demanding moves, ones offering the opportunity for more points from the judges.

Yamaguchi skated well in her short program, as did her closest competitors. The long program or free skate proved to be error-filled for the women. Yamaguchi slipped while landing from a jump and touched the ice with her hand to keep her balance. The ice was even less forgiving for Harding and Ito, however. Both fell during their free skate performances. Consequently, after years of practices, competitions, and performances, Yamaguchi had achieved her dream of winning an Olympic gold. Only four other women—Tenley Albright, Carol Heiss, Peggy Fleming, and Dorothy Hamill— had stood on the top of the Olympic medal award platform for the United States. Yamaguchi was now counted among an elite, special group of American women athletes, earning a special place in Olympic history.

It had been a long and exciting journey for Kristi Yamagu-chi, a child of Asian parents who endured life in Japanese intern-ment camps during World War II. It had also been a challenge: Kristi was born with deformed feet—not the best circumstances in which to aspire to be a competitive athlete. She also had a burning desire, though, to succeed and achieve her dreams. Yamaguchi dared to dream the grandest dream of all—to be an Olympic gold medalist—and saw her dream come true. It was not an easy journey, rather one filled with endless hours of practice, hard work and gritty determination. Yamaguchi's story is one of inspiration; it demonstrates that if you have a dream, you should go for it, and not let doubt, physical challenges, or anything else deter you from realizing it.

2

Asian-American Heritage

Kristi Yamaguchi believes she is no different than the millions of Americans who live within the countless cities and towns across the United States of America. It is only her ethnic heritage as an Asian American that further defines her as a member of a distinct group. The United States is an unusual country in that most of its citizens are not indigenous, or native to the country. Eminent American poet Walt Whitman (1819–1892) wrote of America in his preface to *Leaves of Grass*, "Here is not merely a nation, but a teeming nation of nations."

In actuality, the United States was created by the immigration of many different groups of people, from countries including Great Britain, Germany, Ireland, Scotland, Italy, Russia, China, Japan, and Africa. There were native peoples already living in America before the first European explorers stepped upon her shores, but it is generally accepted that America as a country was founded by immigrants whose arrival began in 1607 with the founding of the Jamestown settlement in Virginia. It was during this period that the African slave trade also flourished. Though involuntarily brought to America, about 500,000 African Americans contributed to the country's population by the time of the American Revolution. The various groups came for many reasons, including political freedom, religious tolerance, and the hope of economic opportunity.

Between 1830 and 1890, about 7.5 million immigrants came to the United States from various parts of Europe, including Scandinavia, Canada, and China. Many arrived in New York's harbor by boat, passing the Statue of Liberty (1886), the American symbol of freedom and opportunity, before being processed at Ellis Island. The potato famine in Ireland (1845–1851) brought more than 200,000 Irish immigrants to America. In the 10 or so years from the 1840s to the 1850s, the United States accepted 1.5 million immigrants into the country. Though most immigrants living and working during the period before World War I were of European origin, a wave of Asians, mostly Chinese, came in the mid-nineteenth century. This was a time when Americans pushed west to settle in relatively untouched and not-yet-developed lands, where opportunities abounded. Fueled by the California gold rush, many Chinese peasants came to America searching for economic success. For most, panning for gold never brought the wealth they had hoped for, so they took low-paying jobs in the burgeoning mill and factory industries.

Perhaps better known is the part Chinese labor played in the completion of the transcontinental railroad, the ambitious project that linked rail travel from Omaha, Nebraska, to Sacramento, California. More than 10,000 Chinese immigrants helped construct the railway over six years, from 1863 to 1869. Despite their contributions to America's progress, the Chinese were not really accepted. Fueled by rising anti-immigration sentiment, in 1882, the U.S. Congress passed the Chinese Exclusion Act, preventing any Chinese without family in America from entering the country.

THE JAPANESE COME TO AMERICA

The Chinese Exclusion Act represented the first major re-striction placed on free immigration in United States history. Further, it could not be viewed in any other way than what it was—discriminatory and racially restrictive. Ultimately, U.S. immigration laws were modified, but unlike their European counterparts, the Chinese Exclusion Act prevented the Chinese community's growth and assimilation in America.

Unlike the Chinese, who were able to emigrate freely to other countries, the people of Japan had been forbidden by their country's laws to travel to foreign lands. Beginning in 1639, for two centuries, Japan was blanketed in a veil of mystery under a policy of isolationism from the Western world. All that changed when United States naval officer Matthew Perry and his fleet ar-rived on Japan's shores in 1853. At the end of months of negotia-tion with Japanese emissaries, a trade treaty was signed between the two nations, opening Japan to the rest of the world. Though emigration was still illegal, a few hundred Japanese began mak-ing their way to Hawaii and California, working as contract farm laborers. Finally, in 1884, the Japanese government relaxed the law and permitted Hawaiian planters to legally recruit Japa-nese workers.

The Japanese who wanted to leave their homeland to work elsewhere referred to themselves as *dekaseginin*—labor-ers working temporarily in another country. Their goal was to go to Hawaii under a three-year agreement for nine dollars a month, plus food, housing, and any necessary medical treat-ment. These contract laborers wanted to earn enough money to return to Japan to either buy land themselves, regain land lost to debtors, or pay off other debts incurred by the family. Because of the exchange rate between the Japanese yen and the American dollar, Japanese laborers could earn six times more

Kristi Yamaguchi's grandparents made their living on farms in California, like these Japanese-American workers picking peas on an Alameda County farm in 1942.

a day working on a Hawaiian plantation than they could on a farm in their own country.

With the opportunity for better wages, Japanese immigration to Hawaii and the West Coast mainland of the United States swelled. From 1885 to 1924, more than 200,000 Japanese came to work in Hawaii, and 180,000 traveled the rest of the way to the West Coast, finding work mostly in California. Pay on the

U.S. mainland seemed even more desirable, as the promise of a dollar a day (equal to more than 2 yen) could amount to 1,000 yen for a year's work—almost as much as the yearly income of the governor of Japan! Many Japanese came to Hawaii to fulfill

Between the Generations

HISTORY OF JAPANESE EMIGRATION

The first people to emigrate from Japan did so mostly because of economic pressure. They came from the southwest regions of Yamaguchi, Hiroshima, and Kumamoto. During the Meiji era (1868–1912), the new emperor of Japan pursued an ambitious plan to put his country on the same economic and military plane as the Western powers. To fund this bold program, Meiji imposed annual taxes on land but kept the price of rice low, causing great economic hardship on the farmers. Pushed to find the means to earn more and pulled by the promise of higher wages in Hawaii and the United States, the first immigrants came more because of economic necessity than a curiosity about the world beyond their isolated one.

Most of the first immigrants came to Hawaii under three-year contracts. Despite harsh working conditions and being exploited for the cheap labor they provided, most stayed through the duration of their contracts. The Japanese had little competition—Chinese immigration had been halted in 1882. Emboldened by the demand for laborers, the Japanese fought for higher wages and better working conditions. Eventually, many earned enough money to open their own businesses. By the 1940s, about 40 percent of the merchants in Hawaii were Japanese.

The second wave of emigrants from Japan, who arrived on the shores of California, came between 1890 and 1907. Though some traveled on from Hawaii, most came from the poor southern provinces of Japan. Farmers by trade, the Japanese soon were producing almost 10 percent of California's farm crops. Working the their dream of earning good money to help the families they left behind, and once they became used to the higher wages and increased opportunities, they found it difficult to imagine returning to their home country.

land, they turned swamps and arid ground into productive farms, introducing crops such as strawberries, celery, and even certain flower species.

The Japanese immigrants saw themselves as separate and distinct from their children. To distinguish one from another, divisions between generations were given terms—Issei, Nisei, Sansei, and Yonsei. The Issei had been born in Japan and had come to America between 1890 and 1924. They were Japan's pioneers in the United States. Their children, or Nisei, were born in America between 1900 and 1940. The third generation Japanese Americans, or Sansei, are the offspring of the Nisei.

The Issei had been raised in a culture that emphasized loyalty, traditionalism, and duty to country and family. They spoke little English and often felt like strangers in an unknown culture whose values seemed alien and difficult to understand. They took labor-intensive jobs that required little knowledge of English. Their children, born into and educated in America, had much less difficulty adjusting, speaking the language, and making a greater push toward assimilation into "American" society, even though they lived among those still clinging to their more familiar and comfortable Japanese culture.

Today the Sansei and Yonsei are as American as their Irish, German, and African-American neighbors. They speak English, go to ballgames, play sports, and watch fireworks on the Fourth of July. Though they do not forget their heritage, they want to be accepted and represented in all aspects of society.

KRISTI'S FAMILY EMIGRATES

The story of Kristi Yamaguchi's family's arrival in America is not very different from that of countless others who came to the United States in the hopes of finding a better, more prosperous life. The country of Japan is made up of thousands of islands, with Honshu, Hokkaido, Kyushu and Shikoku being the four largest. Located in East Asia between the North Pacific Ocean and the Sea of Japan, the archipelago's (group of island's) geographic neighbors include Russia, China, and Korea. Japan is about 3,900 miles (6,276 kilometers) from Hawaii, about 1,000 miles (1,609 km) farther than if traveling from Hawaii to California. It is not an easy or relatively quick journey by ship, yet thousands upon thousands of Japanese made the trek.

Kristi's maternal great-grandparents, Koma and Kamekichi Kobata, left Wakayama, a coastal city located at the mouth of the Kinokawa River on the island of Honshu, in the early 1900s. They settled in the Los Angeles, California, area and became flower growers. The place they left, Wakayama Prefecture (a governmental unit similar to a state in America) is situated amid forests that cover three-fourths of the land. It is also the location of three sacred sites in the Kii Mountain Range, linked by pilgrimage routes to Nara and Kyoto, two of Japan's most ancient cities. The sacred sites, situated amid streams, rivers, and waterfalls, echo the blending of Shinto (worship of nature and ancestors) and Buddhism (an Eastern religion based on the teachings of Siddhartha Gautama, known as Buddha).

The Yamaguchis, Kristi's fathers' parents, also left Japan in the early 1900s. They emigrated from Kumamoto, a city on the southern island of Kyushu, an area made lush and fertile by the once mighty Mount Aso. Mount Aso's crater, which extends 11 miles (17.7 km) by 15 miles (24 km), is the world's largest volcano and can be seen only from the air. As one Web site described the area: "It anchors an island rich with minerals and dense with foliage and wildlife that abuts the choppy waters of the East China Sea and the Ariake and Yatsushiro Seas, with the Amakusa Islands out in the distance on one side, and the Inland Sea, which according to Japanese mythology contains islands, 3,000 of them, that are the oldest part of the country, on the other."

ANTI-JAPANESE SENTIMENT TAKES ROOT

The homeland from which the Japanese emigrated was undergoing many changes under the "enlightened rule" of Emperor Meiji. He wrestled control from the *shogunate* (general's administration); theirs was a feudal government in which the population was divided into hierarchical classes—samurai (warriors), farmers, craftspeople, and traders. Meiji then opened Japan to trade with the United States and Great Britain and began to attempt to transform Japan into the Western powers' economic and military equal.

To prevent a takeover of Japan by other nations, Meiji instituted many innovations to maintain independence and block any outside attempts at interference in the country's governmental affairs. The emergence of Japan as an aggressive, imperial nation committed to expanding the country's power and influence in its neighboring countries was not well received elsewhere in the world. Author Harry Kitano wrote, "Japan's appetite for domination threatened the Western powers and fostered suspicion of the Japanese immigrating to North America."

Japan's aggressive posture made it difficult for those who emigrated to the United States to be accepted. Shortly, the place where Japanese immigrants chose to live and work would mean the difference between freedom and confinement. Life in the Territory of Hawaii was vastly different than that on the U.S. mainland. In Hawaii, most of the inhabitants were of Asian descent, and Japanese made up more than 40 percent of the total population. There was very little white working-class presence on the island. Most disputes were over working and living conditions on the plantations. The Japanese accepted low-paying jobs and were exploited by companies in America that relished cheap labor. Still, in Hawaii and America, the Japanese made more money than they did back home.

Although the Japanese who came to the United States in the early part of the twentieth century accounted for less than one percent of the total immigration population at that time, trumped-up news stories in the press painted the Japanese unfavorably. Ill treatment of these foreigners was more personal, more racially driven. Unfounded suspicions that the Japanese were coming to America not to work but to help prepare an attack on the United States were fueled by politicians and journalists. The threat became known as the "Yellow Peril" and led some to encourage the restriction of Japanese immigration. Because the Japanese were labeled enemies of the American workforce and a threat to the country's security, and scorned for being different, rabid racial discrimination against them thrived.

Something else was happening with the Japanese immigrants that had not occurred with their Asian counterparts. By 1930, the percentage of second-generation (Nisei) Japanese almost equaled the number of first-generation (Issei) Japanese immigrants. Of all Japanese immigrants in America, more than 40 percent made the United States their permanent home. They didn't as readily return to Japan; they were creating a Japanese community in America. Most were farmers. Of the 54,000 Japanese gainfully employed in America in 1925, 46 percent were working in some capacity in the agricultural field. By 1940, almost 50 percent of the agricultural workforce on the West Coast was composed of Japanese immigrants. The Japanese also opened businesses—restaurants, barber shops, hotels, laundromats, and medical and legal support services, which provided jobs, goods, and services to the Japanese community living in America. It was the Issei who came to America to provide a better life for their American-born Nisei children, a life they hoped would include being accepted into "American society." It was a reasonable hope, one held by many strangers who came to America's shores in search of a better life.

3

Early Obstacles

For the Japanese living in America, hope for acceptance was quickly dashed on the morning of December 7, 1941, when the Imperial Nation of Japan launched a surprise attack on the U.S. Naval Fleet stationed at Pearl Harbor, Oahu, Hawaii. At that time World War II had been raging in Europe and the Pacific for more than two years. Although Japan, Germany, and Italy had formed an Axis alliance against Great Britain, France, and Russia, expanding the extent of another world war, the United States had not yet entered the conflict.

That all changed on what had been a quiet Sunday morning on the tropical island of Oahu. At 7:53 A.M., a squadron of 183 Japanese planes, including dive bombers, torpedo bombers, and high-level bombers, attacked. The attack left 2,403 dead, 1,178 wounded, and 640 missing in action. All eight of the naval fleet's battleships were either crippled or sunk. It was the worst individual assault carried out against America in its 165-year history.

The Japanese attack on Pearl Harbor, Hawaii, in 1941 caused a wave of anti-Japanese sentiment in the United States.

The attack not only thrust America into its second world war in 27 years, but it also created a swell of rage, fear, and more intense suspicion of the Japanese living in Hawaii and on the West Coast of the United States. This created an instant crisis for the entire Japanese-American community, one that had burgeoned in the short time of emigration. According to the 1940 United States Census, 126,947 Japanese Americans, of which almost 63 percent were citizens by birth, were living in the United States. In addition, 157,905 were living in the Territory of Hawaii.

Immediately after the attack on Pearl Harbor, the Federal Bureau of Investigation (FBI), the federal law enforcement agency that investigates violations of federal criminal laws, arrested more than 2,000 eminent Issei. Hysteria engulfed many of the politicians, journalists, and anti-Japanese organizations throughout the United States. They were calling on President Franklin Roosevelt to order the removal of all inhabitants of Japanese ancestry from Hawaii and the West Coast.

Roosevelt weighed the information and advice given to him about taking such an action, and eventually agreed. On February 19, 1942, he issued Executive Order 9066, declaring the "evacuation" of all persons of Japanese ancestry from the states of California, Washington, Oregon, and Arizona. Though there were calls for Hawaii to do the same with its Japanese population, which by 1942 composed 33 percent of the total population, it did not force their evacuation or removal. With about six day's notice, more than 110,000 Japanese individuals, 70,000 who were American citizens, were instructed to pack only those belongings they could carry. Evacuees had to sell most of their possessions—homes, cars, businesses, furniture, and if things weren't sold in time, they just had to leave these possessions behind.

Tom Hayase, an evacuee, explained the experience this way: "It is difficult to describe the feeling of despair and humiliation experienced by all of us, as we watched the Caucasians coming to look over our possessions and offering such nominal amounts knowing we had no recourse but to accept whatever they were offering because we did not know what the future held for us."

Evacuees reported to civil control centers, where they were registered and given a family "number." This number was written on tags and then attached to luggage and clothing. They didn't know where they would be going, but most complied with the law. After being processed, they boarded trains to take them to 16 assembly centers known as "temporary camps," where they were settled from March until mid-October 1942. These camps were located on fairgrounds or racetracks, where up to a few thousand people could be crammed into one building. Some lived in horse stables. Places where farm animals lived at one time, Japanese families inhabited then. There were no beds, and living conditions were deplorable.

One detainee described what it was like: "It was like a family of 3,000 people camped out in a barn. We lined up for mail, for checks, for meals, for showers, for washrooms, for laundry tubs, for toilets, for clinic service, for movies. . . . Day and night camp police walked their beats within the center."

When the more permanent camps were ready, the Japanese were put on 171 trains, 500 to a train, and taken to one of 10 internment camps. These camps were set up in remote desert areas, where the harsh temperatures and dry dusty terrain made life even more unbearable. Camp locations were Amache (Colorado), Gila River (Arkansas), Heart Mountain (Wyoming), Jerome (Arkansas), Manzanar (California), Minidoka (Idaho), Poston (Arizona), Rohwer (Arkansas), Topaz (Utah), and Tula Lake (California).

Once at the camp, individuals were assigned to barracks, with each barrack measuring about 20 by 120 feet (6 by 36.5 meters). The barrack was divided into four or six "rooms," with each family occupying an area only about 20 by 20 feet (6 by 6 m). Each room was furnished with a pot-bellied stove, one electric light in the ceiling, and an Army cot and blanket for sleeping. The camps were more like rundown prisons—guard towers and barbed-wire fences defined their parameters.

The interned Japanese lived a meager existence. Their known way of life was suddenly gone, their very freedom seized in an instant. The internees utilized government-owned or -leased farmland to produce poultry, eggs, and pork. Some locations also produced beef and dairy products. It cost about 45 cents per day to feed each camp resident. At each sitting, 250 to 300 people were fed, cafeteria style, in crowded conditions. Workers earned an average of $16 per month for a 44-hour week; they found it almost impossible to save money.

During internment, some Japanese were allowed to leave the camps—to work, to attend college, and to serve in the military. Many Nisei wanted to show their patriotism and loyalty to America, so in early 1943, Secretary of War Henry Stimson announced plans to form an all-Japanese American combat team from volunteers on the mainland and Hawaii. Of the approximately 12,000 who volunteered, more than 4,000 Nisei enlisted and reported for military training at Camp Shelby, in Mississippi. The resulting military unit became known as the 442nd Regimental Combat Team. Shipped off to Italy in May 1944, the 442nd fought fiercely and honorably, earning the distinction as one of the most decorated units in U.S. military history.

KRISTI'S FAMILY AT THE CAMPS

Included among those residents at the Poston, Arizona, camp were Kristi Yamaguchi's father and his family. Jim was just four years old when he and his family were forced to leave their ranch in Gilroy, California, and relocate to the internment camp. Three years later, when they were permitted to leave Poston, a church group helped the Yamaguchis go to Santa Maria, California. While they got back on their feet, things were so tough that they lived in a tent.

Poston was large (71,000 acres), so it was divided into three separate camps. Those interned there were relocated from Southern California, Kern County, Fresno, the Monterey Bay Area, Sacramento County, and Southern Arizona. At its peak population, Poston held more than 17,000 internees. Situated in the desert, Poston was probably the hottest and most uncomfortable camp of the 10. In summer, the temperature could reach 115°F (46°C), and the wooden and tarpaper barracks offered no real shelter from the heat. Poston had 611 males eligible for military service, all of whom joined the U.S. Army. All were assigned to the 442nd Regimental Combat Team. Twenty-four Japanese men from Poston died serving a country that had interned them in a "prison" camp.

Several hundred miles away, in Colorado, Kristi's maternal grandmother Kathleen Doi, was trying to make the best
of her living situation at the Amache internment camp, in the
southeastern part of the state. The first internees to arrive at
the camp came from the Merced Assembly Center on August
27, 1942. Most of the internees had been uprooted from cities
and towns along the Northern California coast, West Sacramento Valley, Northern San Joaquin Valley, and Los Angeles.
At its peak population, more than 7,000 Japanese Americans
lived at Amache. While Kathleen was enduring life at Amache,
her husband, George, who was born in America, was serving as
a lieutenant in the Army. He had been an engineering student
at the University of Southern California when the war began,
and he fought with his infantry division in Europe.

While George was in Europe fighting for America, Kathleen
"voluntarily" went to the camp because no one would rent her
a room and she was concerned about her safety. If that weren't
enough to handle, Kathleen also gave birth while at the camp.
Her daughter Carole, born in 1945, was one of 5,918 babies born
to imprisoned parents. That baby girl would one day marry Jim
Yamaguchi and give birth to her own daughter Kristi, in freedom, nearly 30 years later.

Although President Roosevelt rescinded Executive Order 9066 in 1944, the last internment camp wasn't closed until March 1946. The financial and emotional losses of being
detained were inconceivable. Some estimate that the Japanese
evacuees had no choice but to leave behind approximately $200
million in commercial and personal property when they were
sent to the camps. Despite the pain, suffering, and humiliation
inflicted by the U.S. government, most of the interned Japanese
remained in the United States, determined to start their lives
again. The blemish on America's history remained unrecognized
for 46 years, until the United States government officially acknowledged the travesty against those interned, offered a formal
apology, and provided a $20,000 token financial restitution to

GO FOR BROKE!
THE 442ND REGIMENTAL COMBAT TEAM

"No loyal citizen of the United States should be denied the democratic right to exercise the responsibilities of his citizenship, regardless of his ancestry. The principle on which this country was founded and by which it has always been governed is that Americanism is a matter of the mind and heart; Americanism is not, and never was, a matter of race or ancestry."

These were the words of President Franklin D. Roosevelt on February 1, 1943, when he officially activated the 442nd Regimental Combat Team. The team was made up of *Nisei*—American-born sons of Japanese immigrants to the United States.

The 442nd's motto—"*Go for broke!*"—described the bravery and determination of each of its members. The 442nd fought valiantly in eight major military campaigns in Italy and France during World War II. It earned 18,143 individual decorations, including a Congressional Medal of Honor, 52 Distinguished Service Crosses, and more than 9,486 Purple Hearts. The 442nd became one of the most decorated units in the history of the U.S. military.

Among the members of the 442nd was Second Lieutenant Daniel K. Inouye, who lost an arm while leading his platoon in an attack on enemy positions. He later received the Distinguished Service Cross for his bravery. Inouye was elected to the U.S. House of Representatives in 1959 and to the U.S. Senate in 1962, where he still serves. He was the first American of Japanese descent to serve in either house of Congress.

In 2003, in a letter to a girl who had visited him in Washington, D.C., Senator Inouye spoke about what had happened to Japanese Americans like him during World War II. "Please remember that the story of my experiences during World War II is—by itself—not important," he wrote. "Much more significant are the values that the 442nd Regimental Combat Team and other segregated units represented: that patriotism and love of our great country are not limited to any ethnic group, and wartime hysteria must never again lead us to trample on our democratic principles."

each family affected by Executive Order 9066. Today, a monument stands at what once was the Poston Relocation Center. On it is inscribed the following quote:

> This memorial is dedicated to all those men, women, and children who suffered countless hardships and indignities at the hands of a nation misguided by wartime hysteria, racial prejudice, and fear. May it serve as a constant reminder of our past, so that Americans in the future will never again be denied their constitutional rights, and may the remembrance of that experience serve to advance the evolution of the human spirit.

World War II raged in Europe and the Pacific for six years. In March 1945, the Allied Forces (the United States, Great Britain, and Russia) began their final assault on Germany, forcing the surrender of Germany and Italy on May 2, 1945. On the other side of the world, Japan continued its fierce battles in the Pacific, but the country was losing badly. Recognizing that Japan would fight to the very end rather than submit to unconditional surrender, the U.S. military command decided against an invasion of mainland Japan. Based on many other battles, particularly one very brutal and costly one on the island of Okinawa that resulted in a high number of casualties, ground combat was not seen as an option. Wanting to limit casualties and bring the war to a speedy conclusion, the United States decided to drop two atomic bombs on Japan—one on Hiroshima, the other a few days later, on Nagasaki. On August 10, 1945, Emperor Hirohito announced the surrender of Japan to the Allied Forces, bringing an end to World War II.

In early 1944, the Japanese interned at the 10 designated camps during the war began to be released from their confinement. Official declaration of the end of confinement came on December 17, 1944, when the United States War Department announced "the revocation (effective on January 2, 1945) of

During World War II, U.S. citizens of Japanese ancestry were considered threats and were relocated to centers. Kristi Yamaguchi's father and his parents were sent to the relocation center in Poston, Arizona (*above*).

the West Coast mass exclusion orders, which had been in effect against people of Japanese descent since spring 1942." The Allies' progress in the war contributed greatly to the timing of the revocation. By 1944, even though the war still raged in Europe and the Pacific, the Axis Powers (Germany, Italy, and Japan) were losing badly. The United States no longer saw the interned Japanese as a threat to the nation's security. In actuality, over the duration of World War II, only 10 people were convicted of spying for Japan. All of them were Caucasian.

Although detainees began leaving the camps in 1944, the last camp, Tule Lake Center, wasn't closed until March 20, 1946, well after the effective date announced the year before. The previous December (1944), the U.S. Supreme Court had ruled that the War Relocation Authority (WRA) did not have the authority through Executive Orders 9066 and 9102 to subject U.S. citizens who avow their loyalty to detention in internment camps. (The WRA, established by Executive Order 9102, empowered the agency to "provide for the removal from designated areas of persons whose removal is necessary in the interests of national security." The WRA was further empowered to provide for evacuees' relocation and their needs, to supervise their activities, and to provide for their useful employment.) Some viewed the Supreme Court decision to be too little too late, as about one-third of detainees had already left the camps.

LIFE AFTER THE CAMPS

What did it mean to the more than 100,000 Japanese who had been interned to return home? Internee Aya Nakamura described what it was like after being away from his home for six years:

> Finally getting out of the camps was a great day. It felt so good to get out of the gates, and just know that you were going home . . . finally. Home wasn't where I left it though. Getting back, I was just shocked to see what had happened, our home being bought by a different family, different decorations in the windows; it was our house, but it wasn't anymore. It hurt not being able to return home, but moving into a new home helped me, I believe. I think it helped me to bury the past a little, to, you know, move on from what had happened.

Many of the Nisei were just anxious to get on with their lives, even if that meant having to start over. The internment deeply affected all those who endured confinement, discrimination, and humiliation as a result of "relocation," but it was the Issei who had the most difficulty returning to a "normal" life. Many were bachelors and had no one to return to. There was fear of the un-known, fear of not being able to make a living, even fear of pos-sible hostility from the locals in their new neighborhoods. Many of the interned had grown elderly during confinement. They were ailing and in need of the medical attention and assisted care they received in the camps. Where, though, would they find shelter and assistance on the outside? Going back to life as it was before evacuation and relocation was virtually impossible.

Many detainees were returning home without knowing what they would find. The least fortunate returned to find their homes owned and occupied by another family or razed to make way for more development, their farms auctioned off because of back payments, or even their stored possessions stolen or vandalized.

There were also some happier stories. Those fortunate enough to have someone who had looked after their properties and businesses returned to find them still functioning and in some cases even flourishing. There were the stories of the Cau-casians who helped their Japanese American friends and busi-ness associates, who didn't buy into the racial bias and hysteria promoted by their democratic government. Still, thousands of former interned Japanese struggled to regain any semblance of normalcy beyond the barbed wired and makeshift barracks that had been their prison-home for so long.

REBUILDING

Like many other Japanese families evacuated from California, the Yamaguchis and the Dois went home to the San Francisco Bay area and to Los Angeles as quickly as possible, to begin their "after internment" life. Initially, the Japanese did not re-ceive much help from the United States government, which gave each family (via the WRA) $25 in cash and a bus or train ticket back home.

The internment had severely disrupted the Japanese work-force. Many men who fished for a living before the internment found it difficult to go back to work, because their boats and equipment had been seized, or they had received only pennies on the dollar for their gear. Without enough money to repurchase boats and gear, the best they could hope for was a job as a deckhand. Returning soldiers fared a little better; they could take advantage of the G.I. Bill, which would pay for their college education, allowing them to learn new trades and skills before seeking employment.

Kristi's grandparents once again grew flowers, did gardening and landscaping, and tried to get back into farming. In an interview, Carole said that her father wasn't bitter about the internment. Kristi never heard her parents talk much about that dark time in their lives. Carole was actually too young to remember. Jim just wanted to look toward the future and not to dwell in the past.

The couple met while in college. After studying to become a dentist, Jim served as an Air Force captain in the 1960s. He was stationed in Okinawa. It was the first time he had been to Japan. After graduation, Carole took a job as a medical secretary for two doctors. Jim and Carole later married and lived in Haywood, California, before moving into a brick-and-stone home in Fremont, a city south of San Francisco on the eastern side of the San Francisco Bay. Their first child, Lori, was born in 1969. Two years later, a second daughter was born, whom they named Kristi. The petite little girl, who weighed 5 pounds, 15 ounces (2.7 kilograms) at birth, arrived on July 12, 1971. Rounding out the family, a son named Brett was born three years later.

CULTURAL BALANCING ACT

Neither the Yamaguchis nor the Dois taught their children to speak Japanese, so Jim and Carole grew up without learning the language of their families. Although the Yamaguchis did not speak the language, they did instill Japanese heritage in their children. Each child was given a Japanese middle name to honor that heritage. Kristi was given the middle name Tsuya (pronounced "TSU-ya"), which was her grandmother's name. While raising all three children, Jim and Carole tried to provide exposure to Japanese and American traditions, customs, and holidays. This proved to be a difficult balancing act.

Kristi wore a kimono, a traditional garment of Japan, when she had the chance. Kristi explained, "I remember every year at school when they had United Nations day. Kids would go to school dressed up. My sister and I always wore our kimonos." The kimono (the word means "something worn") is an ankle-length garment worn by Japanese men and women. It has full sleeves and a V-neck, lapped left over right across the chest. It is secured at the waist by a broad sash, called an obi. The gown comes from the Early Nara period (645–724) and is still worn today.

Kristi and her siblings were exposed to their Japanese heritage, but they were also raised like most other American kids. They celebrated Halloween, with costumes and trick-or-treating in their neighborhood. They watched in gleeful fascination as colorful fireworks burst overhead on the Fourth of July. They also hunted for eggs at Easter and exchanged gifts at Christmas. The Yamaguchi kids played outside, rode bicycles, played ball, ate American foods, and spoke English.

Aside from the fact that they looked a bit different than their Caucasian friends, Kristi and her siblings were just typical American children. In an interview given before the 1992 Winter Olympics, Carole described just how American her children were: "[M]y kids never even dated Japanese kids. My oldest dates a Jewish fellow. . . . You know, they're fourth generation; they're so assimilated. They don't speak Japanese. I think they speak more French."

AN EARLY CHALLENGE

Although Kristi was a bright-eyed happy, healthy newborn, her parents noticed that there was something unusual about her feet. Instead of pointing forward and out, they were point-

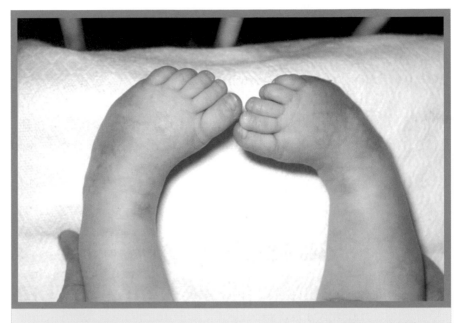

Kristi Yamaguchi was born with club feet or talipes, a birth defect in which one or both feet are twisted out of position.

ing in and curling under. Any attempt to realign or straighten the feet by hand was futile. Kristi had, in fact, been born with clubbed feet, a birth defect that affects about one baby in every 300 born. Twice as many boys as girls are affected, and though physicians are not sure what causes the condition, it is treatable.

Jim and Carole took two-week-old Kristi to an orthopedic specialist for evaluation and treatment, which usually involves three different aspects—undergoing physical therapy and wearing corrective shoes and a specially designed brace while sleeping. Before Kristi could even do that, though, casts manually set in the correct position were put on her feet. Without treatment, Kristi would have never been able to walk correctly, let alone skate.

The leg casts kept Kristi's feet from moving back to the inward, curling position. Recasting Kristi's feet was required every two weeks, to improve their position. This process went on until Kristi was nine months old. Once the casting phase was completed, Kristi began the second part of her treatment. The worst part was wearing the brace when she went to sleep. "I remember the brace, because it hurt so bad," she told author Shiobhan Donohue years later. Slowly, the infant learned to "wobble" walk, until she gained her balance. Jim and Carole watched with hope and concern as Kristi struggled on her feet.

Kristi's early physical challenges didn't slow her down, however. As a toddler, she behaved like her peers, bustling about, curiously exploring her world. As a preschooler, Kristi discovered the arts, falling in love with ballet. The dance lessons also served as a way to help Kristi strengthen her legs. Exposure to dance would also serve Kristi well in her future success because the training would provide a terrific foundation for the choreography and graceful movements that are an integral part of figure skating performance. Carole was thrilled because anything Kristi did where she could use her legs only helped her overcome her early physical condition. Her sister, Lori, was also taking ballet and tap lessons.

FALLING IN LOVE WITH A SPORT

Lori soon found her passion—baton twirling—and eventually went on to compete nationally. She even won a world title as a member of the San Jose Cruzers. Of course, Kristi had to try twirling too, and she performed in a parade with her sister. It was Kristi's first experience performing for the public. Kristi tried many different activities, including playing basketball in a league where her father served as the coach of her team, and even cheerleading. She found her passion, however, in a most unlikely place—the Southland Mall (near San Francisco). The batons, pom-poms, and basketball were suddenly laid silent.

One day, Carole took Kristi with her to the local mall to do some shopping. At the mall was an ice rink, where local skaters would often put on ice shows. On this particular day, the Yamaguchis came upon one such performance. Once Kristi's eyes locked onto the glittering costumes the skaters were wearing, and she watched as they gracefully glided along the ice, she knew she wanted to do that, too. From that day forward, she begged and begged Carole to let her skate, but her mom was concerned that her daughter was still too young and the sport too dangerous for a four-year-old.

In her autobiography, *Always Dream*, Kristi described how she finally got to lace on a pair of skates: "We saw more ice shows, and I kept begging to skate. 'When you start school and can read, then we'll see,' mom promised. I came home from my first day in first grade and announced: 'I can read! Now can I go skating?' Mom kept her promise." Kristi's passion and determination would become assets later on, as she began to train to be an Olympic champion.

4

For the Love of the Ice

Kristi was challenged by adversity at birth, so perhaps that is why she didn't seem to be daunted by much that many other kids her age might have found intimidating or scary. She approached everything with such enthusiasm and joy that it is not surprising that she embarked on her first ice-skating encounter in the same way. Her desire to lace up a pair of skates and step onto the ice for the first time was almost a fulfillment of her destiny. When asked years later about how she felt about being out on the ice, Kristi said, "When I'm skating I feel like I can do anything: I feel like I can stay out there forever."

The first time Carole took Kristi to the skating rink, she worried about how her daughter would fare on the ice. "I remember the first time she put on skates. . . . She had a difficult time because she was very small and not very strong," Carole recalled. Kristi's first outing at the rink included a neighborhood boy her age, his mother, and Kristi's mother. On a rented pair of skates, Kristi stepped onto the ice and did have some trouble standing, so Carole just skated behind Kristi and held her under the arms to help her balance. Kristi had the time of her life, gliding around and around the rink, laughing and smiling as she skated. For some reason, when it was time to leave the ice, Kristi thought the skates were now hers to keep and refused to give them back. She didn't understand that she was only borrowing them. For the longest time, whenever she went back to the rink, she always asked for "her" skates.

SOMEDAY THAT COULD BE ME

Once Kristi realized her dream of skating on the ice, she expanded her dream to include skating in a professional ice show. She loved to dress up in costumes and was excited about wearing the very kind of glittery outfits she had seen the performers wear. She was getting more time to skate by then, and she had the opportunity to watch the televised performances of the best figure skaters in the world as they competed in 1976 at the XII Winter Olympic Games in Innsbruck, Austria. The two-week, sports-filled extravaganza was an exciting time in amateur athletic competitions. Although Innsbruck represented the twelfth time the Winter Games had been held, a few new events were introduced for the first time at those Games, including the beautiful precision skating called ice dancing. The figure skating events—pairs, men's and women's singles, and ice dancing—offered five-year-old Kristi Yamaguchi a chance to see beautiful costumes and entertaining choreographed performances on the ice.

The United States had three entrants in the women's singles competition. The best hopes of a gold medal win came from a shy 19 year-old named Dorothy Hamill, who did go on to win the gold medal in the women's singles competition at Innsbruck. Her grace, athleticism, and beauty on the ice mesmerized the judges and won her the adoration of figure skating fans around the world, and she was an instant celebrity. In *Always Dream*, Kristi recalled how she didn't really quite understand what the Winter Olympic Games were all about. Yet, after watching Dorothy Hamill skate, Kristi knew from watching the reactions of the people on the television, and Dorothy looking so happy, that Hamill had done something special.

Kristi felt an instant connection with Dorothy, and she became the young girl's role model. Kristi's friends were even talking about the United States' new gold medalist, recalling that Kristi did something like that, too. "I remember friends talking about Dorothy Hamill and saying, 'Hey Kristi, you ice skate, don't you?'" she said.

Dorothy's achievement and popularity thrust her into the spotlight. Soon she was swarmed with endorsement offers. She appeared on magazine covers and cereal boxes, and she even had a doll in her likeness on the market. Kristi loved dolls. She had so many on her bed that Kristi had little room for herself when she climbed in to go to sleep at night. A few months after the Olympics, Kristi received her very own Dorothy Hamill doll as a gift. All the dolls Kristi owned were special, but this one was something beyond special: Outfitted with a costume like the one Dorothy wore at the Olympics, the doll also had a little gold medal around its neck and tiny ice skates on its feet.

Kristi's mom wasn't surprised that her daughter took the doll everywhere, even when she began taking skating lessons at the Southland Mall rink. Kristi put on her skates and wobbled over to the entrance to the ice, holding tightly to the wooden railing that wound around the rink. Sometimes Kristi left her Dorothy doll sitting on the edge of the rink so it could "watch" her practice. Eventually Kristi felt brave enough to let go of the railing and glide in a kind of herky-jerky move along the ice. Sometimes she even took the doll with her, lowering it to the ice so the little skates could glide the doll along with Kristi while she "skated."

Dorothy Hamill, shown here winning the gold medal in the 1976 Winter Olympic Games, was an inspiration to many young skaters, including Kristi Yamaguchi.

LEARNING THE BASICS

Kristi's first lessons were actually group lessons with other wobbly, wide-eyed children about her age. At first, Kristi cried whenever they were en route to the rink because the idea of going into a group of kids she did not know frightened her. She didn't like to have to skate across the rink or through another group of kids also taking lessons, but with a different instructor. Once she stepped onto the ice, though, Kristi's fears disappeared and she was able to enjoy herself. In the beginning, Kristi fell down a lot. All the kids did. Over time, though, the group demonstrated the ability to stay up on their skates. Then it was time for them to learn the basic moves of ice skating—spinning, crossovers, spirals, skating backwards, and even jumping.

The first jumps are like the bunny hop—skipping along the ice from one foot and landing on the other. There are six major jumps to master in figure skating—axel, salchow, toe loop, loop, flip, and lutz. Jumps can be executed individually or in combinations. Some of the jumps are performed by pushing off on the edge of the skate; others are achieved by "toe-picking," or taking off with a toe assist, digging the front toe pick on the skate into the ice.

Often, the skater will spin or twist while airborne and successfully complete the jump by landing back down on the skate blade cleanly. These jumps need to be mastered if one has any desire to make it to the competition level. Some of the moves are named after the skaters who created them, like the axel, the lutz, and the salchow. Axel Paulsen was a Norwegian figure skater who is credited with creating the most difficult of jumps. The axel is the only jump where the skater takes off from a forward position on the ice. Many of the moves and jumps in figure skating are quite challenging and not easy to learn. It takes hours and hours of practice, in which the skater tries the move over and over again.

TAKING THE NEXT STEP

Kristi learned quickly, and by the time she turned six, she was ready for her own coach. She started working with a woman named Ann Cofer. Twice a week, Kristi and her mom would get up often before sunrise to get over to the rink for two hours of practice skating before the school day began. Kristi had the perfect build for a skater. She was short, compact, and petite—a great combination for jumping. Cofer provided Kristi with what she needed—structure. She asked her young pupil to keep a log from every practice, encouraging Kristi to write down what she did during each session. An entry from her journal dated February 20, 1981, in *Always Dream* illustrated how Kristi broke down her entry—Jumps, Spins, and Footwork, and how many of each type of jump and spin she accomplished.

When Kristi entered skating, compulsories (school figures) were a required part of any competition. School figures were a way for judges to evaluate how well an ice skater controlled the edges of the blades on each skate. This demonstrated the skater's overall technical skills. Skaters were given a "figure" or set pattern, like the popular figure 8, to trace on the ice using a prescribed part of the blade edge. Once finished, a judge would examine the "figure," checking the cleanness of the pattern and its depth. Obviously, if the pattern had traces of etched ice outside the main figure, points were deducted. As tedious and boring as mastering compulsories was, Kristi knew it was as important as the jumps, spins, and footwork in her skating programs.

In 1978, at the age of seven, Kristi entered her first local skating competition. Kristi skated at an Ice Skating Institute of America competition in their Freestyle 2 event. Freestyle events range from levels 1 to 10. A freestyle event is a program routine that is set to music and emphasizes the required test level maneuvers from the skater's current freestyle level. The event requires various skills, depending on the test level. Kristi was young and new to skating, which worked in her favor. Not surprisingly, she won her first gold medal. Of that day so long ago, she recalled how she hadn't been sure what winning the gold medal in her category meant other than the fact that her parents were very excited for her and lots of people were taking her picture.

Even though she was focused on skating, Kristi was still just a normal kid with her own joys as well as fears. Her brother Brett nicknamed Kristi "Cricket" because she was terrified of any kind of flying or crawly insects, and was especially afraid of spiders. She admits to having had nightmares as a child, needing to leave her bedroom door ajar so she could hear the sound of her parents watching television to help her drift off to sleep.

DOROTHY HAMILL

In 1956, U.S. women's figure skater Tenley Albright won the Olympic gold medal in the Winter Games at Cortina d'Ampezzo, Italy. Five months later, on July 26, future gold medal winner Dorothy Hamill was born in Chicago, Illinois. Soon after her birth, parents Carol and Chalmers Hamill moved the family (which included an older brother and sister) to Riverside, Connecticut. Dorothy's first experience gliding around on the ice occurred on the frozen pond behind her grandparents' house in Greenwich. It was the desire to learn how to skate backward that prompted Dorothy to ask her parents for skating lessons, so at age eight, the future Olympian began her amateur skating training.

Dorothy's exceptional skating skills became apparent quickly. Hamill knew immediately that she had found her life's passion. She told author Sam Wellman, "I wasn't particularly athletic or gifted, but I loved it. I'd be at the skating rink all day long, just skating around and around. I could be all alone and nobody could get near me and I didn't have to talk to anybody. I was in my fantasy world." By age 14, she was so immersed in the sport that

Even the children's fantasy classic *The Wizard of Oz* scared Kristi. She was terrified of the flying monkeys and the Wicked Witch and covered her eyes with her hands when such scenes came on the screen. Count Kristi out if you want to go see a gory movie, too. She refused to watch them as a kid, and won't watch any of them to this day.

NEW COACH, NEW CLUB

Kristi went through her first competition without fear of performing in front of a crowd or a group of judges, so it seemed clear that she was comfortable with that part of the sport. She was willing to work hard, as evidenced by her

she stopped attending school and opted to be tutored privately, so she could devote hours a day, seven days a week, to her skating. The turning point in her career came when she began to train with internationally renowned skating coach Carlo Fassi, who had coached Peggy Fleming to an Olympic gold medal in 1968. It was with Fassi's skillful guidance that Dorothy created the kinds of skating routines that exhibited her athleticism and grace on the ice, including her Hamill Camel spin (a camel spin that moved into a sit spin).

Though she always suffered from terrible nerves before stepping onto the ice to perform, Hamill won the hearts and admiration of fans worldwide when she skated for the gold medal at the 1976 Winter Olympics in Innsbruck, Austria. She set a new fad among young girls all over America with her signature hairstyle. She also earned accolades from competitors and judges for the balance of athletic skills and ballet-like dance grace she seemed to execute almost effortlessly in her figure skating. A three-time Nationals champion, Olympic gold medalist, and World Figure Skating champion during her amateur career, Hamill is considered one of the best freestyle skaters to ever lace up a pair of ice skates.

early-morning sessions and the time she dedicated to practicing her skating. Kristi then joined the Palomares Figure Skating Club. Palomares had its first club session at the Southland
Ice Arena in Hayward, California, in 1973. In time, the club
became an official member of the United States Figure Skating Association (USFSA), the national governing body for the
sport of figure skating in America. The USFSA is recognized
as the official governing body by the United States Olympic
Committee and the International Skating Union (ISU). According to its Web site, the function of the USFSA is to "provide programs to encourage participation and achievement in
the sport of figure skating. Among other things, the USFSA
status as governing body gives it the authority to regulate and
govern the sport in the United States, create rules for the holding of tests, competitions and other activities, and to organize
and sponsor competitions for the purpose of stimulating interest in the sport."

While Kristi participated in a summer skating camp in
her hometown area, she had the good fortune to meet Christy
Kjarsgaard, one of the San Francisco Bay area's top figure skating coaches. Kjarsgaard was all too familiar with the figure
skating world; she knew what it took to be competitive. She
started skating at age five, the age Kristi was when she had
seen her very first ice skating performance at the Southland
Mall. Kjarsgaard was a good figure skater, and she moved up
the ranks, skating in competitions throughout her childhood
years. She was skilled and talented enough to reach the U.S. National Figure Skating Championships. While in college at the
University of California at Berkeley, Kjarsgaard started working with other skaters, teaching them the nuances of the sport.
When she graduated in 1974, Kjarsgaard decided to make full-
time coaching her career.

Twenty-seven-year-old Kjarsgaard certainly believed that
Kristi had potential. In *Always Dream*, Yamaguchi recounts that
Kjarsgaard said of her student, "Kristi has a great work ethic,

great perseverance, and great ability. She made each day like a competition, so that when she got to a competition, it was like a practice. She was very focused. She had a goal each day."

Despite Kristi's enthusiasm and interest in becoming a competitive skater, though, Kjarsgaard wanted to make sure the Yamaguchis and their daughter understood the journey on which they planned to embark. Kristi would need hundreds of hours of lessons that could cost $80 an hour. She would need to be able to set aside countless hours of time for practice and purchase hundreds of hours of ice time at $200 an hour. She'd need professional-quality equipment, including skates that cost $300–$500 a pair—ones she would grow out of quickly.

Kristi's parents not only had to be willing to make the financial commitment, but they'd have to make time sacrifices, as well. Kjarsgaard wanted Kristi at the rink by 5:00 A.M. That meant Kristi and Carole would have to rise at 3:45 A.M., so Kristi had enough time to gobble down breakfast and have her mom drive her to the rink to meet Kjarsgaard on time. It was a difficult pace for Carole and Kristi to maintain. After skating for five hours, Carole then had to drive Kristi to school. Kristi often was in bed before the sun went down in the evening, and her schoolwork could not suffer because of her skating. It was a lot for an eight-year-old to manage, but Kristi so loved what she was doing that no sacrifice was too great, no difficulty too challenging.

Under Kjarsgaard's tutelage, Kristi knew she might be able to realize her dream of learning how to skate so well that she could perform in a professional ice show. Christy Kjarsgaard could certainly be the one to help her young charge reach her goal. Beginning in 1976 and almost every year afterward, Kjarsgaard had the distinction of coaching least one skater who appeared in either the U.S. or Canadian Nationals Championships. Could she coach Kristi into becoming a championship-level competitor?

5

Jumps, Spins, and Pairs

Unlike many of her nine year-old peers, Kristi didn't have the luxury to do fun things after school and on weekends. Once she committed herself to the hours required to undergo the rigors of training and practice sessions necessary to make it as a competitive figure skater, Kristi's time was pretty much divided just between school and skating.

One time, Kristi was forced to take some time off from skating, although it was not to do something fun. As a growing and maturing nine-year-old, Kristi's mouth was just too small for all her teeth. After an evaluation, it was determined that 10 teeth— 6 baby teeth and 4 permanent teeth—had to be extracted. Even though Kristi's father Jim was a dentist, he didn't want to be the one to cause his little girl any pain, so the Yamaguchis took their daughter to an oral surgeon.

In *Always Dream*, Kristi says the extraction of her teeth was the most physically painful experience of her young life. Initially, she thought getting all those teeth pulled would be no big deal, but when she woke up from the sedation, she thought she was dying because the pain was so great. The swelling and cotton ball dressings over her stitches gave her "chipmunk cheeks," but that only lasted about a week. What was the best part of the ordeal? Kristi cashed in big with the Tooth Fairy, who left $10 under her pillow in exchange for the teeth that she had safely stored in a plastic tube under the same pillow the night before. The downside to the ordeal, besides the pain, was that Kristi had to take off two weeks from skating while her mouth healed. It was probably the longest Yamaguchi has ever been off the ice.

MORE THAN GLIDING ON THE ICE

Though Kristi disliked going to sleep at night while it was still light outside, she never minded waking up at 4 A.M., because she always looked forward to getting to the rink to work with coach Kjarsgaard. Kristi loved to learn new things, and Kjarsgaard was only too happy to teach her eager young student. There were 42 different compulsory figures to learn, many jumps of varying difficulty to master, and a diversity of spins and twirls to conquer on the ice. Kristi had to learn all that, while skating gracefully with all the different types of spins, moves, and jumps incorporated into one skating program choreographed to music.

Most skaters love to jump and spin in the air, and Kristi was no different. What no one liked was falling onto the ice. Not executing a jump properly and landing awkwardly on your skates caused you to lose your balance, resulting in a fall that was usually painful. Falling wasn't always a bad thing, however. Two-time United States Olympic gold medalist and figure skating commentator Dick Button once said, "Falling down is not the sign of a poor skater, but the sign of a skater who never stops trying to improve."

To be a good skater, you had to learn the subtle differences in what part of the skates to use to perform a certain type of move. The great figure skaters, the successful ones, not only learned what skate edge to use for which jump, and when to use the toe pick, but also how to execute them well, getting the takeoff and landing timing exact, all without having to think about each part of the process. The more complex a skating jump, the greater the difficulty factor in learning the maneuver. In order of difficulty, the jumps to master are the toe loop, the salchow, the loop, the flip, the lutz, and the axel. In a sport where grace and artistic style are often overridden with what at times seems more like acrobatics and gymnastics than skating, both skills are necessary to be a complete, viable skating competitor.

Figure skaters have been trying to perfect complicated jumps for decades. Most skaters can master a single jump with relative ease. It's when other things are added in that the process gets more difficult. For example, a jump and a twirl in the air before landing is more difficult than executing a simple jump-off-one-foot-and-land-on-the-other-foot maneuver. Mixing two different types of jumps in one move is even more difficult. A skater's airborne time is just seconds. The biomechanics of jumping can be explained as follows.

A skater can progress from a single, to a double, to a triple, and now even to a quadruple jump, but he or she must either jump higher or rotate faster, or somehow combine both techniques. The skater uses the time added by the increase in jump height to complete the required number of revolutions. In addition to meeting the minimal height and rotation speed requirements to complete the jumps, skaters must also be concerned with their horizontal speed. A skater must have enough speed to glide out of the jump into his or her next trick, without breaking the fluidity of the program. In addition, judges are more impressed by jumps performed at fast speeds with great heights and jump distances, so these usually result in better marks for the skater.

JUMPS AND SPINS

Toe jumps (toe loop, flip, lutz) are all executed using the toe pick on the front of the skate blade. For example, the toe loop is accomplished as the skater glides backward on the outside edge of

Skater Dick Button, shown competing in 1948, created and perfected jumps that still challenge skaters today.

the right skate and jabs the left toe pick into the ice, then rotates the body to the left. Because of the ease of this jump, it is often incorporated at the second half of a jump combination. To do a lutz, the skater uses the left outside edge of the skate blade and jabs the right toe pick into the ice. Skaters are often confused when beginning to learn these maneuvers, because he or she has to remember which toe pick and which edge to use while executing a particular jump.

Edge jumps are executed when the skater takes off from a particular edge of the skate, without the advantage of using the other skate. Using the toe pick to push off is not permitted. One edge jump, called the salchow, is completed as follows: The skater takes off from the left back inside edge, then turns counterclockwise on the ice. He or she stands on the left leg, settles into that left back inside edge, and then scoops the right leg up and over the left to begin the jump rotation. The axel, the only jump executed in a forward takeoff motion, ends backward like all the other jumps. Trying to perform more than one rotation in this jump is what makes it very difficult.

Skaters can choose from a number of spin moves, but speed, the number of rotations, and control are most important to judges when they look at a move. The most well known spin, the Scratch Spin, or Corkscrew, is usually seen at the end of a skate program. When executing this move, the skater is standing up straight, with his or her legs crossed and arms overhead or in front of the body, as he or she turns in place. The camel spin is a variation on the scratch spin. In this move, the skater stands on one leg and holds the other leg and torso parallel to the ice. The flying camel (invented by Dick Button) is another variation in which the skater jumps in the air before settling into the spin. Kristi's idol, Dorothy Hamill, created her own camel spin, aptly named the Hamill Camel. The skater starts out in a camel spin and then moves into a sitting position or sit spin, which is executed by bending one leg while extending the other out in front of the body. The lower the skater can "sit" on the bended leg, the better the spin.

Figure skaters have been pushing athletic competition to the extreme for a long time. Skaters who combine difficult jump maneuvers increase the difficulty factor for high scoring from the judges. Whenever a skater successfully introduces a more difficult jump, pressure is put on the rest of the competitors to equal the difficulty of that jump in their program. The first triple jump (a triple loop) ever executed in competition was achieved by Dick Button at the VI Olympic Winter Games in Oslo, Norway, in 1952. The first triple axel wasn't executed in competition until 1978 (by Vern Taylor of Canada), when Kristi was just seven years old. Kristi wouldn't see anyone accomplish a quadruple jump until she was among the top-ranked skaters in the world, nearly 10 years later.

TAKING ON PAIRS SKATING

All of the hours Kristi practiced and was coached were showing in her continual improvement as a skater. Kristi enjoyed it tremendously. She impressed her coach enough in 1982 that Kjarsgaard felt Kristi was ready to participate in an official USFSA competition. At only nine years old, Kristi was entered into the competition in the pre-juvenile division of the Central Pacific Regional Championships. Kristi was nervous, but she had skated well: She performed a single lutz and two single jumps in her free skate program. She was judged on both her compulsory figures and music-accompanied free skate program, and she came in fifth place. Had she finished just one place higher, she would have advanced to the Pacific Coast Sectional Championships, which takes the top four finishers from each of the Regionals. The last challenge is to finish in the top 4 of the 12 competitors in the Sectionals competition, which earns a trip to the National Championships.

That year would be an important year in Kristi Yamaguchi's skating career. In July, Kristi entered the Chabot Skate, a USFSA-approved, nonqualifying competition open to qualified skaters from all over America, Mexico, and France. The Palomares Figure Skating Club, of which Kristi was a member, hosted the event. Kristi skated in the category that included 11-year-olds and came in first place. That fall, the 1982 Central Pacific Regional Championships turned out to be just as exciting for Kristi, as she moved up to the juvenile level and competed as a "seasoned" 11-year-old, placing fifth overall.

This time at the Central Pacific Regionals, though, Kristi met Jim Hulick, another figure skating coach in the San Francisco Bay area. He coached Rudy Galindo, a 13-year-old Mexican-American skater, who needed a pairs partner. Rudy was small for his age—he was just 4'6" tall and rather thin. Part of skating in pairs competitions requires the male to lift his female partner in the air and launch her into "toss jumps." Because of his size, Rudy needed to find a partner he could handle. Kristi fit the bill. Hulick spoke to the Yamaguchis to see if he could train Kristi and Rudy in pairs skating. The Yamaguchis just wanted their daughter to be happy, so they left the decision

FIGURE SKATING COMPETITION LEVELS

Before a figure skater takes to the ice at an amateur televised event, he or she has to compete against a host of other skaters—skaters who television viewers never see—at other competitions. They are all vying for the top spots, which will allow them to advance to the next competition level. By the time a skater competes at the World Championships, he or she has had to participate in three previous competitions and finish in the top three at each of those events in order to qualify for the next level.

There are two types of competitions: nonqualifying and qualifying. In nonqualifying competitions, winning does not make the skater eligible to skate in another competition. Winning or placing in a defined spot does offer eligibility to skate in qualifying competitions, however. In the skating world, the United States is divided into Sections—East, Midwest, and Pacific Coast. Each section has three regions, thus there are nine regions in the country. The first stage in America's qualifying competition for the U.S. Championships is the Regional championships. The Regionals are held up to her, provided her schoolwork did not suffer because of the added skating responsibility. Kristi had seen Rudy on the ice and thought it would be fun to work with another skater, so despite coach Kjarsgaard's reservations, Kristi decided to try training for both singles and pairs figure skating.

With the added pairs skating training, Kristi was now skating in the morning with Kjarsgaard and meeting with Rudy and Hulick for an hour each afternoon after school. Pairs skating has its own difficulties and challenges. Both skaters need to do their movements in sync or in unison, so timing is critical and requires hours of practice. Skating together with someone else on the ice so close to you has its dangers, too. A mistake or a mistimed move might result in one skater falling and possibly

annually each fall. The top four finishers at each Regional event qualify to compete in the Sectionals. The top four finishers at each Sectional event qualify to compete in the U.S. Nationals championship. Just making it to the Nationals is an achievement worthy of celebration.

Making it to the World Championships, however, is an even more unlikely proposition for even most competitive skaters. Each International Skating Union (ISU) member nation can enter one skater or team in each event, and some countries, including the United States, can send up to three participants (usually the first-, second-, and third-place finishers at the Nationals). The Worlds are the most prestigious competitions in all of figure skating. Only the top skaters from around the world come to compete against each other, to vie for the title of world champion. In 1991, the United States women finished an astonishing 1, 2, and 3, with Kristi Yamaguchi capturing the gold, Tonya Harding the silver, and Nancy Kerrigan the bronze, a feat not accomplished before or matched since.

being injured in the process. When the skate program is executed properly, though, pairs skating can be a beauty beyond expectation.

Kristi was especially concerned about the "Death Spiral," a dazzling but unnerving maneuver on the ice. The female skater is spun around her pivoted male partner while only holding one hand. The female lowers down backward, stretching away from her partner on one skate until her head is just inches above the surface of the ice. In *Kristi Yamaguchi*, author Sam Wellman described the appearance of the "Death Spiral": "When performed correctly, the death spiral made it appear that the man was pulling a woman up from the edge of a cliff: she would spiral down toward the ice and then the man would lift her up slowly until she was standing on her own once again."

GAINING MATURITY AND LEARNING ARTISTRY

Kristi and Rudy grew up together, almost like brother and sister; they skated as pairs partners for seven years. At times, Rudy lived with the Yamaguchi family, and he and Kristi traveled the world together competing in pairs events, while Kristi also competed in singles competitions. At each practice, Kristi and Rudy got better at skating together, and Kristi continued to improve her own individual skating skills.

The now-teenage competitor had always set her sights on one day competing in the Nationals. So far in her young competitive career, Kristi had come close to finishing high enough in the Regionals to move on to the Sectionals, but had not yet broken through the qualifying round. Skating had long ceased to be just an enjoyable hobby for Kristi. She had developed the will and the drive to be a competitive, dominant athlete in her sport and realized that she would need to devote even more time to attain her goals. It didn't take long for Kristi and Rudy to move up from novice to junior division pairs skaters and for Kristi to move up to novice skater in the singles category.

Fourteen-year-old Kristi was finding it increasingly difficult to juggle school, two skate-training schedules, and travel to competitions, so she asked her parents if she could stop attending school after finishing eighth grade. She would instead study with a private tutor at home. Despite their reservations, Jim and Carole Yamaguchi recognized how skating had changed from being part of their daughter's life to being her main focus. They agreed to allow Kristi to work with a tutor, as long as she continued to keep up her educational training.

Still, getting beyond the Sectionals was going to be a challenge. There were the compulsories to master, something Kristi dreaded. She needed to mature artistically, to learn how to feel and interpret music in her skating to a choreographed program. Skating in competitions was more involved than just training, practice, and executing jumps and spins. Kristi now had to take on a more active role in her skating: She had to choose her costumes and a theme and music to skate to and develop artistic interpretation.

In the fall, Kristi competed in the novice singles competition at the 1985 Central Pacific Regional Championships, as well as in the junior pairs with Galindo. The pair earned a spot at the Pacific Coast Sectionals, and Kristi did well enough in her singles performance to advance one step closer to the Nationals, too. In pairs, Kristi and Rudy again advanced; they were then on their way to their first Nationals competition. In her debut in the individual skate at the Sectionals, Kristi's artistic program included a few jumps with greater difficulty than she had performed previously—a triple toe loop–double toe loop combination, as well as a triple salchow. When the judges weighed in with their scores, Kristi's total was not only high enough to earn her first place, but it was also her ticket to compete in the 1985 National Championships in Kansas City, Missouri. For American skaters who win medal placements at the Nationals, the reward is a trip to represent your country at the World Championships. National medalists also represent the United States at the Olympics every four years, so Kristi (and Rudy) had a very ambitious road ahead.

GOING NATIONAL AND INTERNATIONAL

Kristi's first National Championships appearance was exciting. She had an opportunity to watch some of the more experienced pairs skaters before she and Rudy skated their program, and Kristi and Rudy finished a respectable fifth place in the juniors division. Even more exciting was Kristi's singles performance— her very first Nationals competition, and she just missed the bronze medal. Her experience at the Nationals gave Kristi the opportunity to see some of the other singles skaters make their mark in the sport as well.

Tiffany Chin, who the previous year, at the 1984 Olympics, had finished fourth, won the Seniors gold medal. Debi Thomas, who later went on to become the first African American to win an Olympic medal (a bronze in 1988), won the silver medal, and Brian Boitano, who later secured his place in figure skating history by winning the men's singles gold medal at the 1988 Olympics and two World Championship titles, took the men's gold medal at the Nationals in 1985. The best of the 1985 season came when Kristi and Rudy were invited to compete in the junior World Championships in Sarajevo, Yugoslavia. It was an honor and a privilege for Kristi and Rudy to showcase their talents before a group of international judges, who scored them well enough to earn the duo a fifth-place finish.

The year 1986 was charmed for Kristi and Rudy. After qualifying for the junior Nationals being held on Long Island, New York, the pair came out in matching dazzling red costumes, astonishing the audience and the judges with their side-by-side jumps and spins. When performed in opposite directions on the ice, these spins gave off a mirror-like effect. The crowd roared at the end of their program. When the final scores were announced, Kristi and Rudy had done the unbelievable—they were the 1986 national junior pairs champions.

Kristi Yamaguchi and her partner Rudy Galindo practice their routine in Paris, France, in 1989, two days before the World Figure Skating Championships.

It was an amazing win, as Kristi and Rudy had only been skating together for three years, and now they were the top-ranked pairs skaters in the U.S. in their division. The win guaranteed a trip to the Worlds, where the pair medaled again, winning the bronze.

Coach Hulick felt his pairs team was ready to move up to the seniors division. Coach Kjarsgaard didn't feel Kristi was ready to move up to seniors level in singles skating though, as she had not yet won a junior division medal. Kristi rectified that at the Nationals, held in Tacoma, Washington, the following year, by winning the silver medal—her first Nationals medal ever. In their first performance in the seniors pairs event, Kristi and Rudy skated well, ending up with a respectable fifth-place finish. At the Worlds in Brisbane, Australia, in 1988, Kristi won the junior women's title, earning her first Worlds gold, and she and Rudy, who dropped back to the junior pairs division, won the gold medal, too. From here on, Kristi would skate in the seniors division, competing with the best skaters at the top of the sport.

SETBACKS OF A RISING STAR

At 16, Kristi had achieved more and traveled farther than most of her peers, and as exciting as it all had been, she felt she was missing out on her some important things in her life. She had been around the world and had become a world champion. Skating had been all consuming, though, and Kristi had no social life outside the rink and the skating world. To feel more connected with kids her own age, Kristi decided to return to school for her junior year, enrolling in Mission San Jose High. It would be tough again to juggle educational responsibilities with her skating demands, but Kristi was a little older and had shown she was able to handle whatever pressures had come her way.

The 1988 season had been a bit of a letdown for Kristi. By skating in the women's singles seniors division at the Nationals in Denver, Colorado, she had hoped to qualify for the U.S. Winter Olympics, to be held in Calgary, Alberta, Canada. Up against the talents of Debi Thomas and Jill Trenary, however, Kristi finished tenth overall. In the pairs competition, she and

Rudy just missed the cut for the Olympics, finishing in fifth place overall. Instead of getting down over the disappointing finishes, though, Kristi was just all the more determined to get back to the rink and train and practice even harder. The following year would be a new beginning, a new chance to make it to the top, and a year of change, successes, and loss. Stepping on the ice at 5:00 A.M. to begin anew with the 1989 Nationals and Worlds in her sights, she couldn't have known what a great year was about to unfold for her professionally, and what tragedies would also test her resolve. Did she have the true heart of a champion? She was about to find out.

6

Achievement and Loss

Although 1988 had its disappointments for Kristi, she did receive her first major acknowledgement as a skater in a form other than medals from competitions. She learned that she was chosen to be the recipient of the 1988 Women's Sports Foundation Travel and Training grant. The Women's Sports Foundation, a charitable educational organization, was founded in 1974 by tennis great Billie Jean King. It is dedicated to advancing the lives of girls and women through sports and physical activity. Each year, several awards, grants, and scholarships are presented to individuals to honor their athletic achievements and recognize individuals for their commitment and dedication to the advancement of women's sports. The grant was quite an honor for Kristi, and it meant a great deal to the aspiring figure skater.

Kristi was able to use the grant to buy equipment she needed to continue to compete, which took some of the pressure off her parents. Supporting Kristi in her skating endeavors was very expensive for the Yamaguchis, not only financially but in their time commitment as well. Their middle child never took any of it for granted, and she always remained grounded and family oriented. In *Always Dream*, older sister Lori shared the same view, saying, "At a certain point in her career, the family focus was on Kristi. Still, she found time to show Brett and me that we were still important to her. I remember my senior cheerleader tryouts. She made a good-luck sign and came to the tryout to cheer me on. She never got too big for her family."

DREAMS CAN COME TRUE

Kristi continued to train hard and dedicated huge amounts of time to her singles and pairs training. She was determined to make 1989 the year she would skate in the seniors division in both singles and pairs. Her goal was to get to the World Championships, in Paris, France. Kristi was also now a senior at Mission San Jose High. Senior year was normally a time for socials, proms, and other special end-of-high-school activities, but Kristi wasn't able to participate in many of the events because her time was so consumed with skating practices and training. Would the hard work and dedication pay off? The first test would be the U.S. Nationals, to be held February 6–12, in Baltimore, Maryland.

Kristi was becoming known in the figure skating world. Just before the Nationals, ABC TV sent a camera crew to tape Kristi during one of her early morning practice sessions with coach Kjarsgaard, then while skating with Rudy in the afternoon. The newscasters even followed her while she was out shopping with some of her friends. The segment was part of ABC's "Up Close and Personal" feature, which aired during the Nationals as a way of introducing some of the competitors to the viewing audience. Though still a rather shy person around strangers, Kristi was used to performing in front of hundreds of people, so it didn't make her uncomfortable to know that millions of people would probably see her TV profile.

RUDY GALINDO

Rudy Galindo's rise in the figure skating world was shared with his seven-year pairs partner Kristi Yamaguchi. Together, they won two U.S. Nationals titles before Yamaguchi decided to focus exclusively on her singles skating. The breakup sent Galindo into a downward spiral before the long road back to a singles National title in 1996.

Born Val Joe Galindo on September 7, 1969, Rudy was the youngest of three children in a Mexican-American family living in San Jose, California. Galindo's journey onto the ice began when he saw his sister Laura skating. He laced up a pair of skates to join her, and it didn't take long to see that pint-sized Galindo had enormous potential. Though he was competitive in singles for his age class, Galindo's real talent emerged when he was paired with Yamaguchi. Despite their meteoric rise, Yamaguchi dropped pairs training, leaving Galindo without a partner. At the time, Galindo was also dealing with the deaths of his pairs coach, Jim Hulick, and brother George. For a while, he stopped skating, preferring to numb his pain by partying, drinking, and doing drugs.

It was seeing Yamaguchi on television winning the Olympic gold medal that finally dislodged Galindo from his self-destructive path; it motivated him back to the ice and to competitive skating. His comeback was complete when he won the U.S. National men's singles title in 1996. Galindo's skating successes have had to share space in his life with many adversities, however, including his HIV-positive diagnosis in 2000 and two total hip replacement surgeries in 2003. Starting physical therapy immediately after the surgeries, Galindo was back on the ice six weeks later. Performing in several ice shows since, Galindo has been able to execute many of the difficult jumps and spins as well or better than he did before surgery. For Galindo, being in front of an audience makes everything he's been through worth it.

Soon the precompetition hype was over, and it was time to perform. Kristi and Rudy took to the ice and skated their short program. They did well and were in second place, behind Natalie and Wayne Seybold, at the conclusion of the short program. Next up for Kristi was her compulsory figures skate in the women's singles competition. Jill Trenary, the Nationals champion in 1987 and second-place finisher in 1988, was the favorite to win in Baltimore. Kristi's school figures were never her strong point, but after completing them and her short skate program, she was in fourth place overall. The pairs long program was scheduled the night before the women's free skate final, so Kristi switched her focus back to her pairs skating with Rudy. Skating to music from *Romeo and Juliet*, Kristi and Rudy completed their triple jumps, as well as the other elements in their long skate program, cleanly. At the end of the 4½-minute performance, announcer Dick Button said, "This program is simply wonderful, absolutely thrilling."

Kristi and Rudy had indeed skated a beautifully artistic and technically masterful program. When their scores were revealed, 5.7's and a 5.8 out 6.0 total flashed on the screen. The Seybolds did not do as well in their long program skate, and their scores were not high enough to hold onto first place in the standings. It took a moment for Kristi and Rudy to realize that they had won—they were the 1989 National Pairs Champions! The win not only meant the gold medal—it also meant a trip to the World Championships in Paris, France. The following evening, Kristi faced the biggest skate of her career so far.

Skating to Jacques Offenbach's "Gaité Parisienne" ballet, Kristi's choreographed program was one of the most technically difficult in the competition. The 17-year-old completed seven difficult triple jumps while maintaining a beautiful artistry in her skating, and she masterfully used the expanse of the rink as her stage. When the music ended and Kristi stood in the middle of the rink to take her bow, she received a standing ovation from the crowd. The judge's scores reflected their agreement with the

Kristi Yamaguchi performs at the World Figure Skating Championships
in 1989. Splitting her time between pairs and singles competitions made
Yamaguchi's solo work suffer.

crowd, awarding Kristi marks of 5.7 to 5.9. On the strength of her short program, Kristi had climbed from eighth after the compulsory figures into fourth place overall. Her commanding skate in the long program catapulted her into second place. Jill Trenary maintained her lead and won the gold medal, but Kristi had realized her dream of winning her long-sought-after medal in the Nationals.

Aside from her silver medal and a place on the U.S. team to compete at the Worlds, Kristi made figure skating history by being the first female since 1954 to win a medal in two events at the Nationals. Back home, her high-school classmates greeted Kristi enthusiastically. Although she did not participate in any varsity sports at Mission San Jose High, the school elected to present Kristi with a letter jacket in honor of her achievements at the Nationals. Said Kristi of the honor, "That jacket meant a lot to me and I wore it proudly at my first Senior World Championships in Paris, France."

DEALING WITH CHANGE

Coach Jim Hulick was proud of Kristi and Rudy. They had risen very quickly in the competitive ranks of skating and had done so with remarkable poise and professionalism. Hulick had been keeping something from the pair, though, and he knew it was time to tell them. He had been sick for a while; he was diagnosed with cancer the year before. Somehow, he managed to keep the news from his young skating pair while he was undergoing treatment for the disease. He decided to tell Kristi and Rudy about his condition after the Nationals. The good news was that Hulick was well enough to travel with the pair to Paris for the World Championships. Hulick was just happy that he would be able to see Kristi and Rudy skate, no matter where they finished. Unfortunately, the Worlds weren't as kind to Kristi or her partner. In pairs, they came in fifth place; in her singles competition, Kristi placed a disappointing sixth.

Christy Kjarsgaard had news, too. While coaching Pauline Lee at the 1988 Winter Olympics in Calgary, Kjarsgaard met Andrew Ness, a physician who specialized in sports medicine. They wed a few months before Kristi's graduation from high school and moved to Edmonton, Alberta, Canada, where Dr. Ness had taken a job. If Kristi wanted to continue to train with Kjarsgaard-Ness, she'd have to move to Edmonton. Finally, graduation from high school was suddenly upon Kristi, and despite the sadness that came with goodbyes to her family and friends, Kristi knew if she wanted to give her dreams a real shot, she'd have to make the sacrifices necessary to make them a reality. Barely 24 hours after graduation, Kristi traveled to Edmonton and moved in with Christy and Andrew.

It was the first time Kristi had ever been away from her family. She began her training with Kjarsgaard-Ness at the Royal Glenora Club, and Rudy and Hulick either came up every few weeks to Edmonton, or Kristi went back down to California so they could continue their pairs training. The schedule was grueling and the stress level high for someone so young. Yet, Kristi was determined. The difficulties were secondary to the goal she had set her sights on—to go to the Olympics and compete in both the pairs and singles competitions. Others who knew Kristi felt she would be able to handle the responsibilities that came with her decision. Hulick referred to Kristi as superhuman. "She has endless strength and natural talent—something no one can teach," he said. Carole Yamaguchi concurred and added that it seemed as though the busier her daughter is, the better she does in whatever she takes on.

Occasionally, Kristi did get homesick. Carole, despite having responsibilities at home with husband Jim and her two other children, visited her daughter in Edmonton as often as she could. It was great when Kristi could spend some time at home with her family, too. That was sometimes even tougher than living away. Kristi explained: "It's hard when I go home and have to leave the next day for a competition. Sometimes I

After Kristi dissolved their partnership, Rudy Galindo (*center*) went on to win first place in the U.S. Figure Skating Championships in 1996.

think, God . . . can't I just stay for a week and get familiar with my room again?" Kristi worked through her homesickness as best she could and managed the frequent trips back and forth to train with Rudy and Hulick. Juggling schedules to cope with the complications of distance was taking its toll on their pairs skating, however.

PERSONAL LOSS AND TRIUMPH

Coach Hulick, who was often in Los Angeles receiving chemotherapy treatments for his cancer, tried valiantly to continue to guide his pairs champions. Kristi and Rudy finished out their 1989 competition schedule with appearances at the Olympic Festival, Skate America, Skate Canada, and NHK Trophy in Kobe, Japan. Although by now Hulick showed signs of losing his battle with cancer, he still accompanied Kristi and Rudy to Japan. It was the last time he would see them compete. The pair just missed taking home the bronze, finishing in fourth place. In the singles competition, however, Kristi took home the silver medal in the women's senior division. Celebration quickly turned to mourning. On December 10, just two weeks after the trio returned from Japan, 38-year-old Jim Hulick died. Kristi and Rudy knew Hulick was ill and had probably sacrificed his health for their skating. His death was a terrible blow to the teens. Kristi honored her former coach by saying, "Our entire career is dedicated to Jim. He started us out and was with us the last seven years of his life. . . . He made us into what we are right now."

Then, just five days later, Kristi's beloved grandfather George Doi also passed away. Doi had always instilled in his grandchildren the importance of working hard and always doing your best. The Dois were Kristi's biggest fans and tried to attend as many of her competitions as they could. Grandpa Doi's passing devastated Kristi. She had experienced her first loss of loved ones and cried for weeks. She had difficulty concentrating on her skating. Soon, though, Kristi realized that the last thing both coach Hulick and her grandfather Doi would have wanted was for her to stop skating.

With the support of family and friends, Kristi returned to the rink. Taking over the enormous responsibility of coaching the pair was John Nicks, a good friend of Hulick's. He offered to help them train to defend their Nationals title in Salt Lake City, Utah, in February 1990. Many wondered if all that had happened would adversely affect Kristi's performance at the Nationals. Because of rules changes that would take effect in July, this was the last time Kristi would have to do the dreaded compulsory figures at the Nationals—and dreaded they were, as Kristi was in fifth place after completing her "etchings" on the ice. Determined not to let the competition slip away, and with it another trip to the Worlds, Kristi skated aggressively in her short program, executing a triple lutz/double toe loop combination that put her right back in medal contention.

For Rudy and Kristi, defending their title was the latest challenge to date in their tremendous pairs career. Despite a fall by Kristi as she was trying to land a triple flip, the pair received 5.8 and 5.9 marks for their performance. They had defended their title and were the 1990 Pairs Champions again. There was really very little time to celebrate, though, because Kristi needed to ready herself for her long program performance. At practice, the wear and tear of the grueling pairs and singles training had obviously taken their toll. She even fell during practice, which was very uncharacteristic for her. That evening, Kristi skated to classical composer Pyotr Ilyich Tchaikovsky's "Swan Lake." Her skating seemed off almost from the start, as she modified a few of her jumps to ones less difficult. As in practice, Kristi fell while trying to execute a triple salchow, and momentarily lost her balance while completing a simple loop. Despite the errors, Kristi scored well enough to earn the silver medal.

After the long skate, Carole, who was concerned that perhaps her daughter had taken on too much, asked Kristi what happened. In *Always Dream*, Carole shared the exchange she had with her daughter: "Kristi broke down and said, 'I wouldn't have fallen down on purpose!' Sometimes we [parents] get caught up in the competition. Parents need to be calm and supportive and always show that we love our children unconditionally." Kristi needed that support at the 1990 World Championships.

Tai Babilonia, seen competing with Randy Gardner in 1980, provided moral support to Kristi before the World Figure Skating Championships.

Support came from outside the family, too. Friend and former Pairs World Champion (with partner Randy Gardner) Tai Babilonia knew of the pressures Kristi would be facing. To provide a little boost, Tai gave Kristi a heart-shaped earring, along with a note, to encourage her. The earring symbolizes hope and strength, and Kristi wore it throughout the rest of her years of amateur competition.

At the Worlds, it became clear that Kristi just wasn't doing the dual training well anymore. She and Rudy finished fifth, and she was bumped out of medal contention by teammate Holly Cook, who took the bronze medal. Kristi's biggest challengers, Jill Trenary and Japan's Midori Ito, took the gold and silver medals, respectively. Kristi's confidence was suddenly shaken. She wondered if she should even continue to skate competitively in singles or pairs. With the Winter Olympics just two years away, Kristi had to decide what she wanted to do. Though torn about what choice to make, Kristi ultimately decided to pursue her career as a singles competitor. Explaining her decision, Kristi said, "The choice was singles, for many reasons. Breaking up with Rudy was terribly sad—like a divorce in the family. We started so young together and had such great plans. But life doesn't always work out as planned."

Kristi recognized that she could no longer skate at the level necessary to be a champion by competing in both singles and pairs; it was a sign that the once dreamy-eyed four-year-old girl had grown up. In order to improve, she knew had to choose. It was one of the most difficult decisions Kristi Yamaguchi had ever made, but it would turn out to be the right move for her amateur career. It was also the only choice to make if she was to have a chance to fulfill her dream of skating in the Olympics in Albertville, France, in 1992.

7

Skating to the Top

Kristi Yamaguchi made the decision to concentrate on her solo skating, but there were times, even many years later, when she questioned whether she had made the right decision when she decided to give up pairs competition. Speaking to an ABC Sports analyst, she shared that doubt: "To this day I still wonder if it was absolutely the right decision, because I miss pairs terribly. There is something about working with someone out there on the ice and having the same goals together."

Rudy Galindo was hurt and angry for a long time, and was upset even more than Yamaguchi by tragedy. He had to deal with the death of coach Hulick, but he also lost his brother George, who died from complications arising from Acquired Immune Deficiency Syndrome (AIDS), and his father Jess, who passed away from heart failure. Eventually, Galindo found his own success as a singles skater, when at the age of 27, he became the first Mexican-American to win the United States Nationals title.

For Yamaguchi to find her own success, she would have to focus all her energies on her skating and turn a blind eye to any distractions. Her first real test came in the height of the summer of 1990. At the Goodwill Games, held in Seattle, Washington, Yamaguchi skated brilliantly and won her first major international figure skating title. She did so in extraordinary fashion, defeating one of her biggest rivals in women's figure skating, World Champion Jill Trenary. At another competition, Skate America, Yamaguchi came in first again, this time holding off her other biggest rival, Midori Ito of Japan. Ito was stellar in her athletic abilities, executing jump combinations few other women, including Yamaguchi, could match. A showdown between the two was likely at the 1992 Olympics. Yamaguchi was expected to excel in the artistic part of figure skating, and Ito's athleticism was guaranteed to wow the crowd and the judges.

ANOTHER RIVAL EMERGES

In 1989, the International Skating Union (ISU) decided that compulsory figures would be eliminated from all competitions by July 1990. As a result, Kristi no longer needed to devote practice time to school figures, which had never been a strong part of her skating and always affected her scores and standings in competitions. With the 1991 Nationals in her sights, Kristi could just focus on her choreography—she could master her jumps and select the music, costumes, and themes to which she would skate. Kristi really believed that through her hard work and more intense focus on singles skating, she had a real shot at winning the Nationals title. She also had one less rival to worry about, as an injury forced Jill Trenary to withdraw from the event.

That February, when Kristi traveled to Minneapolis, Minnesota, she believed she could leave with the gold medal and the National title. Although she skated so well in the short program that it vaulted her into first place, Kristi faced stiff competition going into the long program. Another American, Nancy Kerrigan, was touted as another skater who exuded grace, beauty, and artistry in her skating style. There was also a new, very athletic skater from Portland, Oregon, named Tonya Harding. Word was that she had executed the triple axel in practice. Only Midori Ito had cleanly executed the triple axel in competition, and that had been three years ago. Despite falling while attempting a triple salchow, Kristi received marks from 5.7's to 5.9's. Then Tonya Harding came out onto the ice to skate her long program. About 45 seconds into her skate, Harding completed a triple axel, the first by an American woman. She also landed several more triple jump combinations, and received a standing ovation at the conclusion of her skate. The judges awarded Harding higher marks than Kristi, and with them the U.S. National Title. The order of finish was Harding, Yamaguchi, and Kerrigan.

Kristi was devastated by the second-place finish and admitted to being a mess on the ice during practice for a few weeks afterward. The spirit had gone out of Kristi's skating until Canadian Champion and friend Kurt Browning saw her moping around on the ice and thought he would talk to her. He skated over and just asked Kristi a very simple, yet direct question: "Why are you doing this?" Kristi had to think about the question for a minute before answering that she just loved to skate and couldn't imagine ever stopping. Browning then offered Kristi the advice that turned things around, saying, "Then don't be afraid to smile once in awhile during training. Enjoy it!" From then on, Kristi's outlook changed, and she again found the joy she had for skating that she had lost for a short while.

FINISHING ON TOP

In preparing for the 1991 Worlds Competition, Kristi approached her training with a renewed excitement that was clearly visible to her family, friends, and coach Kjarsgaard-Ness. Browning, going to the Worlds in search of his third straight men's title, even teased Kristi one day when they were driving from practice that there could be two world champi-

In 1990, Kristi Yamaguchi's superb form helped her defeat her two greatest competitors, Jill Trenary and Midori Ito.

ons in the car! For Kristi, Kurt, and the other competitors, the usual precompetition pressures included a lot of speculation in the press about each competitor's chances—who were the favorites to win medals in Munich and what impact the World Championship results would have with the Winter Olympics only 11 months away.

Kurt shook off any pressure he might have felt and turned in a gold-medal-winning performance. Kristi was in the stands the night Kurt skated his first-place program and was thrilled for her friend. Now it was time to focus on her own performances. She skated beautifully in her original program, and was in first place at the conclusion of all the scores. The next afternoon's skate would determine the next world champion. E.M. Swift of *Sports Illustrated* wrote, "Yamaguchi's short program was superb—even Kristi allowed she could hardly have skated it better—and she stood first." Still, she needed to win Saturday afternoon's free skate in order to take home the world title. Not even her mother, Carole, was confident she could do it. "I don't know if she's mentally tough enough yet," Carole said. "And she doesn't have that triple axel."

Finishing first put Yamaguchi in position to skate her long program last in the competition. Such placement could be good or bad, depending on how well everyone else skated. If Kristi was too far ahead in the scoring for anyone to catch her, the title was hers to lose. If someone was close, the pressure would certainly be on Yamaguchi to skate the best program of the night. Tonya Harding and Nancy Kerrigan would certainly be in contention, and Harding had a better mastery of the difficult jumps. It was to be Yamaguchi's night, however. She landed six triple jumps, only missing her nemesis jump, the triple salchow. Despite the fall, her technical merit scores included five 5.9's. It was her artistic scores, however, that thrilled Yamaguchi and Kjarsgaard-Ness beyond words—seven 5.9's and one perfect 6.0, awarded by Italian judge Franco Benini. With that, Kristi was the women's world champion!

From left, silver medalist Tonya Harding, gold medalist Kristi Yamaguchi, and bronze medalist Nancy Kerrigan celebrate after the finals of the World Figure Skating Championships in 1991.

When Yamaguchi realized that she had won, she let out such a shriek of joy that was covered in the press for days after the competition was over. The normally quiet Yama, as Kristi Yamaguchi is called by her friends, caught many people off guard by her outburst. "I'm telling you, you guys don't know her," Kjarsgaard-Ness told some members of the press. "Little, quiet Kristi shrieked." Kurt Browning was so thrilled for Yamaguchi that his face was streaked with tears. The training partners would now indeed share a car ride together as world champions.

Before the medal ceremony, Kristi remarked that it was still hard to believe that she was world champion. It had been a goal, a dream for so long, that it was all almost surreal. With Tonya Harding finishing second and Nancy Kerrigan coming in third, the American women also set a first in Worlds history—a medal sweep by one nation.

TAKING THE NATIONALS TITLE

Winning the World title had been a pressure release for Kristi. Now there were new pressures, and she had to find a way to ignore all the distractions around her as she prepared for the 1992 Nationals—and a potential trip to the XVI Winter Olympic Games in Albertville, France. New programs would have to be created and choreographed, new music selections made, new costumes designed based on a new theme, and Yamaguchi

MIDORI ITO

Nicknamed the "Tsunami Girl" and "Japanese Jumping Bean," Midori Ito had a charisma, charm, and smile that made her a favorite performer to figure skating fans worldwide. The 4-foot-9-inch dynamo will forever be remembered for being the first woman to land the triple axel in a major international competition.

Ito first stepped onto the ice when she was four, and she was skating competitively by the time she was six years old. Success in competition came early, as Ito secured several junior championship titles in 1980. Her seemingly effortless jumping ability amazed judges and audiences. She continued to put the pressure on her rivals when she successfully executed a triple/triple combination—triple toe loop/triple toe loop—at the 1981 Junior Worlds, becoming the first woman in figure skating history to do so at an ISU-sanctioned competition.

The 1988–1989 season was Midori Ito's finest. At the peak of her career, she secured her place in skating history. After winning would have to learn the layout of all her moves, jumps, and spins in both her original and long programs. For her original program, Kristi's music selection was the "Blue Danube Waltz" by Johann Strauss. She would skate her long program to the exotic and powerful "Malagueña," by Ernesto Lecuona. Kjarsgaard-Ness also put Kristi on a weight-training program to build up the muscle strength in her legs.

At the Nationals in Orlando, Florida, in January 1992, Kristi was ready to go. Only the top three skaters would earn a spot on the U.S. Olympic women's figure skating team. Rising to the occasion, Kristi skated two great programs, even landing the dreaded triple salchow. By doing so, she also won a bet with her mom, who used the power of bribery to try to get her daughter past the mental block of the elusive triple jump. As E.M. Swift wrote in *Sports Illustrated* after the Nationals concluded,

her third straight All Japan Championship and the NHK Trophy, Ito electrified the skating world at the Aichi Prefecture. At the 1989 Worlds, she earned two 6.0 perfect marks for technical merit in her original program and six 6.0's for technical merit for her free-style performance. Ito's scores made her the first Asian to win the gold medal.

Although Ito was favored to win the gold medal at the 1992 Winter Games in Albertville, France, the press and the pressure took its toll. Ito fell on the triple lutz in her short program, and although she landed the first triple axel by a woman in Olympic competition, she couldn't overcome her mistakes and ended up winning the silver medal, behind winner Kristi Yamaguchi.

Ito retired from amateur skating after the 1992 Olympics and embarked on a professional skating career in the Prince Ice World shows. At the 1998 Winter Games in Nagano, Japan, Ito ran the first leg of the torch relay, once it arrived in Japan, and she lit the Olympic Torch at the opening ceremonies. In 2004, Midori Ito was inducted into the World Figure Skating Hall of Fame.

Never underestimate the power cold cash has over a financially strapped 20-year-old. Skating to Spanish-style music, at times imagining herself strong-willed and dramatic, at other times soft and romantic, Yamaguchi was pure enchantment on Saturday night. Adding to the drama, Yamaguchi lost her red hairband during a triple toe loop midway through the free-skating program—one of seven flawless triples she landed—in the exact center of the ice, so that each time she skated past it, the spectators' hearts rose to their throats, so fearful was everyone that Yamaguchi might slip on the red ribbon and ruin the performance.

And when Yamaguchi nailed her triple Sal—during the awards ceremony she raised her winner's tray toward her mother and mouthed "triple Sal" to remind her of the $100—her considerable following erupted. That charge gave the final minute of the performance the momentum to crackle to conclusion, with Yamaguchi receiving the most heartfelt standing ovation of the week and a perfect 6.0 from one judge for artistic impression.

GOING TO ALBERTVILLE

On the heels of her first World title, Yamaguchi now had her first Nationals title. More important, she was going to Albertville, with teammates Kerrigan and Harding. Despite Yamaguchi's phenomenal season, she was still the underdog to Japan's athletic dynamo, Midori Ito, who was favored to win the gold medal. Ito's jumping ability still created the buzz in the run-up to the Olympics. Harding could also be formidable with her own jump combinations, although she was not as consistent as Ito. Yamaguchi's idol, Dorothy Hamill, summed up the contrast between Yamaguchi and Ito by saying, "Kristi is graceful and musical, but when Midori skates, she has me on the edge of my seat."

Japanese figure skater Midori Ito, one of Kristi's biggest rivals, performs during the women's original program at the Winter Olympic Games in 1992.

The XVI Winter Olympics opened with the official lighting of the Olympic torch, on February 8, 1992, in the French Alps town of Albertville, France. More than 1,800 athletes representing 64 nations converged on the town to participate in the 57 sporting events that would take place over a two-week period. The mascot for the Albertville Olympics was a half-man, half-star figure named "Magique," which evoked thoughts of dream and imagination with its star-like shape. It was almost too perfect a mascot for 20-year-old Kristi Yamaguchi, who had as a young child set her dream on the Olympics.

Although Yamaguchi would have to wait 11 days for the women's figure skating competition to begin, she arrived early, to participate in the opening ceremonies. Coach Kjarsgaard-Ness's philosophy matched Kristi's and Jim and Carole Yamaguchi's: Being a part of the Olympics is more than just the competition; it's a life experience. What if Kristi were to come away with no medal? What memories would she be left with? Kristi roomed at the Olympic Athletes' Village with teammate Nancy Kerrigan. Together, they kept each other as relaxed as possible and often went to watch some of the other Olympic events together. Kristi enjoyed meeting many athletes from around the world, and she established friendships that would last long after the Games were over.

While in Albertville, Yamaguchi also met a hockey player from the men's U.S. Olympic team—Bret Hedican. A native of Minnesota, Hedican was a multitalented athlete, who, in addition to ice hockey, excelled in football, soccer, and golf. He remembered watching the 1980 "Miracle" win by the U.S. hockey team in Lake Placid, New York, and decided that he wanted to be an Olympian someday, too. Although the U.S. team finished fourth at Albertville, Hedican fondly remembers his Olympic experience and said the greatest moments for him were when he walked into the stadium at the opening ceremonies and then competed in Games. Though it would be three more years before Kristi would see Bret again, Bret never forgot meeting Kristi:

"Obviously she made an impression," said Hedican. "She was a great person then, and still is, but it wasn't until the opening of our new building in Vancouver, G.M. Place (in 1995), that I bumped into her again. I went over and introduced myself, and she obviously didn't remember who I was." Kristi didn't know it at the time, but the 1992 Games would be more important to her life than solely to provide her the opportunity to compete for the gold medal.

When it came time to put the extracurricular Olympic participation aside and concentrate on why she was there, Kristi and Kjarsgaard-Ness knew that the 1½-hour daily practice was not enough to get prepared for the competition, so coach and athlete went to a small ski village called Megève, about 35 minutes outside Albertville, to practice. They couldn't have made a better decision, for it was in Megève, away from the hustle and bustle of activities going on in Albertville, that Yamaguchi found her center and her focus and peaked at the right moment. In an interview with E.M. Swift, Kjarsgaard-Ness recalled, "She skated beautifully in Megève. . . . Prettier than anything I've seen. A step above. I sat her down and said, 'That's all. You don't have to try to do anything more than what you just did.' It was so beautiful, it didn't matter if a panel of judges put her second. That's what I told her. 'If you skate like that, it doesn't matter.'"

THE MOST IMPORTANT SEVEN MINUTES

Finally, the moment had come. Yamaguchi had spent the better part of 14 years of her life practicing, training, and preparing for an opportunity to skate for Olympic gold. Now it came down to seven minutes—2½ minutes for the original program and 4½ minutes for the free skate. How well Yamaguchi skated in those seven minutes would determine whether she would return to the United States as an Olympic champion.

Yamaguchi felt her training had gone well and hoped that all the preparation would equate to smooth performances, where she acknowledged that the gold was not a lock for any one

Kristi Yamaguchi was at the top of her game during the XVI Olympic Games in Albertville, France, in 1992.

competitor. "It's so unpredictable," Yamaguchi said. "No one woman has dominated the field the past four years—we've had three different world champions and three different Nationals champions. Whoever puts on the performance of the year will win it." To provide a personal "good luck" to their daughter, Jim and Carole gave Kristi a special necklace—a heart-shaped ruby-and-diamond pendant. Kristi's choreographer also gave Kristi a note of encouragement, writing, "This is your moment, let it shine."

Yamaguchi stepped onto the ice to skate her original program. She wore a blue chiffon costume decorated in sequins. Re-creating her program from the U.S. Nationals, she skated her two-minute piece to Strauss's elegant "Blue Danube" waltz. She skated a near-perfect routine, with several combination jumps. The judges awarded her seven 5.9's and two 5.8's for technical merit, and several 5.8's for artistic impression. Main rival Midori Ito fell on a combination jump in her original program, placing her in fourth position going into the final round. Yamaguchi was atop the standings, fellow American Nancy Kerrigan was in second, and France's athletic star Surya Bonaly was in third place.

Two days later, Yamaguchi went through her free skate program in front of a crowd of onlookers who were happy to pay just to see her practice. She was halfway to her gold medal win and fulfilling her dream. Yamaguchi didn't want to tempt fate, so when she came across a pamphlet showing what the Olympic medals looked like, she quickly turned the page. She didn't want to get a good look! Heading over to La Halle Olympique that night, Yamaguchi dressed in a stunning, long-sleeved, gold and black costume. As she was getting ready to start her warm-up, someone came to wish her well. She turned around to see her childhood idol, Dorothy Hamill, standing there. Hamill wanted to wish Yamaguchi good luck and to tell her she'd be rooting for her. The visit meant the world to Kristi, and she felt inspired when she finally glided onto the ice.

What happened next was both stunning and a bit unnerving. *Sports Illustrated's* writer E.M. Swift described what
happened:

> Skating first in the last group of skaters, to the Spanish-
> styled "Malagueña," Yamaguchi calmly nailed her open-
> ing triple-triple combination, her ponytail a blur, then
> assuredly turned the ice into her stage. She landed her
> jumps so softly it seemed as if she were skating in her
> slippers. Yamaguchi's program, which was superbly cho-
> reographed by Sandra Bezic, had the crowd spellbound
> until more than halfway through, when she fell—the
> groan!—on a relatively easy triple loop. Her confidence
> shaken, Yamaguchi then turned a planned triple Sal-
> chow into a double. But she pulled herself together,
> landed the difficult triple Lutz and finished well.

Yamaguchi received a thundering ovation from the 9,000
spectators in La Halle Olympique at the end of her performance. Flowers showered the ice. Although she worried about
her one miscue, she smiled and waved at the crowd. The judges'
scores reflected their pleasure at the sheer artistry and elegance
of Yamaguchi's skating program and execution. It was evident
that they loved the artistic impression of her performance—she
received eight 5.9's! Yamaguchi had only to wait to see how the
other competitors skated to learn whether she had indeed skated
the best performance of the year, sealing her victory and being
awarded Olympic gold. Nancy Kerrigan, in second place going
into the free skate, did well, but not well enough to overtake
Kristi for first place. Midori Ito, the favorite, under enormous
pressure to deliver the gold to her country, fell while trying to
execute a triple axel—a jump she had done with such ease so
many times before. Even though she completed the jump later
in her program, she fell short in her scores and was not able to
knock Yamaguchi out of first place.

From left, silver medalist Midori Ito of Japan, gold medalist Kristi Yamaguchi, and bronze medalist Nancy Kerrigan acknowledge their fans during the Olympic medals ceremony in 1992.

LA MEDAILLE D'OR . . .

Once Ito completed her skate, everyone realized that the gold medal was Yamaguchi's. Ironically, Yamaguchi's win was the first by an American since her childhood idol, Dorothy Hamill, had won 16 years earlier. Awaiting her approach to the medal podium a short while later, Yamaguchi was so unprepared for the reality of what she had just accomplished that she wasn't sure what she was supposed to do. For the first time in two weeks she was nervous, really nervous. She asked bronze medalist and roommate Nancy Kerrigan if she'd have to say anything. Who knew? Neither one had been there before. Who cared! Kerrigan nudged Yamaguchi forward when the announcer called out her name over the loud speaker. Yamaguchi congratulated silver medalist Ito and hugged Kerrigan.

As per custom at all the Olympic medal ceremonies, the gold medal winner had the honor of having her country's national anthem played, as the flags of the gold, silver, and bronze medal winners' nations were hoisted up the flagpoles. Standing on the top step, Yamaguchi and her family were beaming with pride as the sound of "The Star-Spangled Banner" filled the Olympic venue. As Yamaguchi stood there, could she have ever imagined that the young girl with a dream so many years ago, whose own family had been interned in relocation camps a half a century before, would now stand proudly as an American Olympic champion? As the saying goes . . . Yes—only in America!

8

A Life Changed Forever

Winning the Olympic gold medal proved life altering for Kristi Yamaguchi. Together with the other medal winners, Yamaguchi skated in an exhibition for the fans, electrifying the crowd with her performance to "I'm a Yankee Doodle Dandy." Then, suddenly, the competition was over, and so ended the XVI Winter Olympic Games. The closing ceremonies were filled with all the splendor and pageantry of the grand event, and with the pressure of competition over, the athletes were able to soak it all in. As with the opening ceremonies, the closing ceremonies were held at the 35,000-seat Théâtre des Cérémonies, a temporary structure built just for the 1992 Games. At the closing ceremonies, the Olympic Flame is extinguished and the Olympic flag is lowered, folded, then presented to the mayor of the host city of the next Olympic Games.

Unlike in the opening ceremonies, when the athletes march in by country, all athletes who decide to take part in the closing ceremonies enter the stadium randomly. It is an opportunity to share the experience with newfound friends in a truly international spirit. Together with roommate Nancy Kerrigan and a bunch of other members of the United States Olympic Team, Kristi went to the Théâtre des Cérémonies to be a part of the closing ceremonies. Hoisted up by one of the male competitors on the U.S. team, Yamaguchi videotaped as many memories as her camcorder could record. Said Yamaguchi of that cold February day, "I'll never forget the Olympics. It's the best experience of my life."

CAUGHT UP IN A WHIRLWIND

Kristi said the Olympics felt so overwhelming, exciting, and unbelievable that she expected she would have to adjust when she returned home. The newly crowned champion was flooded with requests for interviews by radio, television, and newspaper reporters. In *Always Dream*, Yamaguchi said, "In a blink, a whirlwind of fame picked me up and spun my image around the world." The 20-year-old was not prepared for all the attention she received or all the demands for her time.

Yamaguchi appeared on the nationally televised show "Live! With Regis and Kathie"; more than 500 pieces of fan mail arrived at her house weekly; and her face adorned the cover of the March 2, 1992, issue of *Sports Illustrated,* with the caption "American Dream." Yamaguchi's success on the ice translated to financial opportunities off the ice, in the form of product endorsements. Her first contract was with the fabric company Hoechst Celanese. Endorsement deals with DuraSoft contact lenses, Kraft Philadelphia cream cheese, Ray-Ban sunglasses and Evian bottled water soon followed.

Yamaguchi's face was splashed across a plethora of magazines, and her photo appeared on Kellogg's cereal boxes. Being named official spokesperson for the American Lung Association was a particularly special invitation for Yamaguchi, because it had personal significance. "I was pretty close with my grandfather, who died of lung cancer," she explained. "He was a big

Kristi Yamaguchi rides on the shoulders of pairs figure skater Rocky Marval during the closing ceremonies of the Olympic Games. To her right is bronze medal figure skater Nancy Kerrigan.

influence and he made me work harder. It was tough to see him go through the suffering towards the end."

Capping her amateur career, Yamaguchi entertained the hometown crowd, defending her World title with her first-place finish at the 1992 Worlds in Oakland, California. Getting a feel for skating after a lifetime of competitions, she participated in the Tour of Champions with other Olympic skaters, including Nancy Kerrigan and Paul Wylie. The exhibition tour, which made stops in 42 cities, gave Yamaguchi a chance to fine-tune her performance skills and experience—things she hadn't had the time for while she was in training. She saw a Broadway play while the tour was in New York City, toured Elvis Presley's Graceland mansion while in Memphis, and even went dancing at the hot Hollywood, California, nightclub Spago. As a special presidential delegate at the 1992 Summer Olympics in Barcelona, Spain, Kristi got to fly aboard President Bush's Air Force One. While at the Games, she met other successful athletes, including former Olympic gold medal winners Evander Holyfield and Mary Lou Retton.

Being Asian American

AN AMERICAN CHAMPION

Asians have been emigrating to America's shores since the mid-1850s. Although Japanese laborers were not permitted to leave their country legally until 1884, many arrived along the shores of Hawaii and the West Coast of the United States as early as 1869. Asian Americans have made great strides and have successfully taken their place in many aspects of American society, including business, politics, education, entertainment, and sports. Chinese-American architect Maya Lin's design for the Vietnam War Memorial was chosen from among 1,421 submissions; former Secretary of Transportation Norman Mineta was the first Asian-American Cabinet member chosen by a President. Korean-American platform diver Dr. Sammy Lee was the first Asian American to win an Olympic gold medal and the first male to win two gold medals in that event.

When Kristi Yamaguchi won the Olympic gold medal in 1992, she made history on her own by being the first Asian-American woman to do so. As a fourth-generation Japanese American, Yamaguchi couldn't be *more* American. Her family history is never far away, though, as both of her parents families were uprooted from their homes and businesses and interned with 120,000 other Asians of Japanese ancestry during World War II. The only traces of Yamaguchi's Japanese heritage lie in her family name and her unmistakable Japanese-featured face.

Yamaguchi was born in the United States, was raised in an English-speaking home, celebrated American holidays, and ate

DREAMS FULFILLED AND LOSS ENDURED

One of Yamaguchi's biggest dreams was to skate professionally with a tour company. In 1993, she signed a contract with *Stars on Ice* and was excited to be skating with many other stars, including former Olympic medalists Scott Hamilton, Brian Orser, Paul Wylie, Rosalynn Sumners, Kitty and Peter Carruthers, and

American foods, but her Japanese heritage became a subject of talk in the press after her gold medal win in Albertville, France. The instant celebrity whose face donned the cover of *Sports Illustrated* was not flooded with endorsement offers as was her all-American-looking teammate Nancy Kerrigan. Was it because Yamaguchi didn't look the part of an *American* champion?

Yamaguchi didn't let the speculation bother her. She accepted her fair share of endorsements and continued to enjoy the whirlwind of post-Olympics requests for interviews and appearances. Although she just considers herself a Californian, Yamaguchi doesn't shy away from her recognition as a role model in the Asian community. In 1999, *A. Magazine* chose Yamaguchi as one of the 100 Most Influential Asian Americans of the Decade, and in 2002, Yamaguchi was one of five inductees to the Japanese American Sports Hall of Fame.

Yamaguchi has made a few trips to her family's homeland, and she enjoyed learning more about Japanese culture and her own Japanese heritage. Still, she's married to a Caucasian, Carolina Hurricanes ice hockey player Bret Hedican, and has two daughters with very American names—*first* names, that is. In keeping with a tradition her mother Carole started with Yamaguchi and her sister and brother, the skating star gave each daughter a Japanese middle name. That's about as Japanese as Yamaguchi's own kids will be too.

Kristi Yamaguchi points to team member Scott Hamilton as he does a backward flip in the opening act of *Stars on Ice*.

Ekatarina Gordeeva and Sergei Grinkov. During her 10-year affiliation with the tour, Yamaguchi performed with such figure skating giants as Kurt Browning, Katarina Witt, Ekatarina Gordeeva and Sergei Grinkov, Jill Trenary, Jayne Torvill and Christopher Dean, and Lu Chen.

Turning pro was a huge adjustment for Yamaguchi. Although she no longer needed to rise at 5:00 A.M. to get to the rink for practice, the structure of amateur skating was far different than being on tour. In *Always Dream*, Kristi described the change:

Suddenly, my structured life flip-flopped to road chaos. With *Stars on Ice* I travel five or six months a year. I thought life as a pro would be easy. It's not. It takes as much training now as before, and the travel is grueling. We complain about carrying luggage, strange food, and homesickness. Still, when the lights go on and the crowd roars its welcome, there's no place we'd rather be.

One thing that helped Yamaguchi adjust to her pro career was the friendship and camaraderie with the crew and other performers on the tour. Kristi became especially close friends with Scott Hamilton and the Russian pairs husband and wife team of Sergei Grinkov and Ekatarina (Katya) Gordeeva. Yamaguchi had been spared much of the tragedy and loss that life often brings. With the exception of the deaths of coach Jim Hulick and grandfather George Doi, she had been spared the pain of feeling the loss over those close to you for most of her life. Unfortunately, that was about to change.

On the morning of November 20, 1995, Sergei and Katya were on the ice at the Olympic Center in Lake Placid, New York, beginning the day's practice before the evening *Stars on Ice* show. Sergei, a 28-year-old skating star, never mentioned any health problems other than a painful back that he had been nursing over the last few months. He had always lifted 90-pound Katya over his head with ease during their skating maneuvers, but on this fall November morning as he began a lift he and Katya had done a thousand times before, he collapsed on the ice. Suddenly, Sergei was gone, apparently dead from a heart attack. The skating community, pros and fans alike, was in shock. Sergei's sudden death hit the tour company especially hard, and the close-knit "family" closed ranks around Katya and her three-year-old daughter Daria.

Yamaguchi was shaken; she would miss Sergei, who always had a warm smile and a hug for his costars, always lifting

Russia's Ekatarina Gordeeva and Sergei Grinkov, shown here skating their way to a gold medal in the Olympics in 1994, later befriended Kristi when they toured together in *Stars on Ice*.

them up. Now it was Yamaguchi's turn. As a way of offering comfort to Katya, she gave Katya the heart-shaped earring that Tia Babilonia had given her as a symbol of hope and strength at the 1990 World Championships. As a tribute to Sergei Grinkov, the *Stars on Ice* performers dedicated their 1996 season in his memory. On February 27, 1996, Katya returned to the ice for the first time since Sergei's death. Performing at the Hartford Civic Arena in Connecticut and televised by CBS, Katya skated a solo routine in Sergei's memory. Many of the other *Stars* figure skaters also performed that night. Yamaguchi skated a duet with Scott Hamilton for their own tribute to their friend. Sergei might not be with them anymore, but he would never be forgotten.

The sadness felt by the group over Sergei's loss was magnified when Scott Hamilton left the show in 1997 because of illness. Kristi and the rest of the company were rocked again at the thought that they might lose the heart and soul of *Stars on Ice*. Scott remained unfazed and optimistic, however, despite a diagnosis of testicular cancer. He told his friends and colleagues that he'd be back, and after his surgery and chemotherapy treatments concluded, he kept his word and was back on the ice, skating better than ever.

GIVING BACK

Often, people who are fortunate in life want to help others. Athletes are no different than corporate millionaire sponsors, or kids who throw a car wash to raise money for charity. When *Stars on Ice* decided to hook up with the Make-A-Wish Foundation, the experience had a tremendous impact on Kristi Yamaguchi. Many times while performing in a tour city, children with life-threatening illnesses were brought to the arena to watch skaters like Kristi, Scott Hamilton, or Lu Chen practice. Sometimes they even had dinner with the performers and got to see the show.

Kristi Yamaguchi (*left*) skates with Natalie Wills (*center*) and Enrico Ciccone (*right*) in 1997 as part of the "Make-a-Wish Foundation." Wills suffers from a life-threatening disease.

Yamaguchi's experiences with the Make-A-Wish Foundation prompted her to create her own charitable organization, the Always Dream Foundation, in 1996. She explained the process that led to this development in her autobiography: "Those experiences helped me see that we all have the opportunity to make a difference in someone's life. Sometimes a random act of kindness or a word of encouragement is all someone needs. But we can also help by giving to organizations. That's why I started the Always Dream Foundation." One of the most popular Always Dream fundraisers is the Skates in the Park event. In 1997, the event drew 1,700 skaters from the San Francisco Bay area and raised $60,000 for charity.

RENEWING A RELATIONSHIP

Yamaguchi traveled the world, saw many exciting sights, and met fun and interesting people. She was also often asked to make appearances at openings and events to help bring out a lot of supporters. While on tour in Vancouver, Canada, in 1995, with *Stars on Ice,* Yamaguchi was asked to attend the opening of the GM Place Arena, the new home of the Vancouver Canucks NHL ice hockey team. Bret Hedican, the ice hockey player on the 1992 U.S. Olympic team who introduced himself to Yamaguchi while they were both in Albertville at the Games, was also in attendance. He was playing for the Canucks and was there with other members of the team. Yamaguchi recalled the events of that night in an interview she did with Hedican several years later:

> It was pretty funny, because we had a post reception after the big event in Vancouver, and one of my choreographers was with me, and I said, oh, you know, I just met this guy. He was on the same Olympic team. He's like, oh, well he keeps looking over here. He's cute. Why don't you go talk to him? And I was so embarrassed, and, you know, I was back, you know, transported back to grade school.

The party was a big event. Musical guests Shania Twain, Sarah McLachlan, and David Foster all performed. Later, Kristi and Bret got together and spent the later part of the evening talking. This began a relationship that would only deepen over time. Yamaguchi was amazed at herself because she never thought she'd ever be attracted to an athlete. In *Always Dream,* Yamaguchi described her first impressions of ice hockey players:

> Figure skaters usually despise hockey players. First of all, hockey players take precious ice time away from us. The reason I had to get up so early every day was because

Kristi Yamaguchi signs autographs on her bobble-head dolls for fans in 2002 to help raise money for her Always Dream Foundation.

hockey players hogged the ice in the afternoon. Plus, everyone knows hockey players are gross. They spit all over the ice, they are violent, they change in the lobby, and their terrible stink after practice almost makes you sick just walking by them.

Hedican had to get beyond a lot of Kristi's preconceived notions about hockey players if he were going to date her seriously. They also had to overcome the fact that both had chosen careers on the ice that often required them to travel. There were time zone differences to work out so the two could talk to each other. Sometimes, however, they luckily found themselves in the same city.

At the end of the hockey season, Yamaguchi was in Vancouver finishing up a Canadian tour, and she and Hedican spent the week together. They knew that things were getting serious. After about three years of their long-distance dating, Hedican decided to propose. Flying out of a big snowstorm in Vancouver, he made it to California on Christmas Eve 1998. Things didn't go exactly as planned, but it all worked out in the end. Hedican told the story: "I was planning to do it at dinner, but then her sister and her husband decided to join us, so I put it off. Finally, after that, I decided to take her to a restaurant at the top of the hotel that overlooks the city. Then I got down on my knee and begged." The two decided to set the wedding date for the summer of 2000.

A BUSY TIME

The latter half of the 1990s was a very busy time for Yamaguchi. Aside from her touring schedule, endorsements, the foundation's work, and preparing for a wedding, Kristi won the World Pro Championship title in 1996 and 1997, authored two books (1997, 1998), and was inducted into the World Figure Skating Hall of Fame (1999). Kristi's first book, co-authored with coach Kjarsgaard-Ness, was entitled *Figure Skating for Dummies*. She also penned, with writer Greg Brown, *Always Dream*, her autobiography written for children. In 1998, Kristi was bestowed the honor of running one of the last legs of the Olympic Torch relay for the opening of the Winter Games in Nagano, Japan.

On July 8, 2000, Yamaguchi and Hedican exchanged vows in front of 300 guests at the Orchid at Mauna Lani on the Kohala coast of the Big Island of Hawaii. Gerrye Wong of AsianWeek.com described the special day:

> As the 300 family and friends entered the Plantation Estate outdoor wedding site, they were graced by young ladies presenting orchid leis around their necks, Hawaiian style. Under clear blue skies, the couple were joined in a traditional Hawaiian ceremony, beginning with the blowing of the conch and "Oli Aloha" and "Au Makua"

chants to call everyone to bear witness to this sacred event. As Yamaguchi walked down the aisle in an exquisite Vera Wang gown, escorted by her father, Dr. Jim Yamaguchi, she was surrounded by a pastel mélange of flowers lining the pathway and embellishing the giant wedding archway. Special musical tributes were made by vocalist Nohelani Cypriano accompanied by classical guitarist Charles Brotman.

TIME AWAY FROM THE TOUR

Kristi skated with *Stars on Ice* for two more years after getting married, but decided it was time for a break. She had been skating almost constantly for 25 years, and as much as she loved figure skating, she wanted time to do other things. She still kept her "toes" on the ice, however, skating a few special performances, including the January 2003 Divas on Ice. She also served as a Goodwill Ambassador during the 2002 Winter Olympics in Salt Lake City, Utah. Yamaguchi and Hedican also wanted to start a family, and their wishes came true when daughter Keara Kiyomi Hedican was born on October 1, 2003. A second daughter, Emma Yoshiko Hedican, was born on November 17, 2005. In true Yamaguchi tradition, Kristi gave both her daughters Japanese middle names, as her mother Carole had for her, her sister Lori, and brother Brett.

The Hedican girls will have a lot to live up to with two champions in the house—an Olympic gold medal winner mom and a dad whose name will be inscribed on Lord Stanley's Cup. Hedican and his Carolina Hurricanes teammates won their first NHL Stanley Cup championship for the North Carolina hockey franchise in June 2006. It is the first championship for Hedican in his 16-year pro-hockey career. The family celebrated together as the city threw the team a victory party throughout the streets of Raleigh.

Never one to inflate herself, Yamaguchi has always kept her successes and career in perspective. She has never forgotten her

Kristi Yamaguchi and Husband Bret Hedican pose with their two young daughters and the Stanley Cup. Hedican's team, Carolina Hurricanes, defeated the Edmonton Oilers in the NHL Stanley Cup Finals in 2006.

family and her roots, and she still has heroes all these many years later—like the four-year-old Kristi who made Dorothy Hamill one of them so long ago. When asked about her heroes, Yamaguchi says she needn't look any farther than her parents. In the closing of her autobiography, she said:

> What can I say to parents who love, support, and encourage me? What can I say about a mother who gave up her career to keep me on the ice? What can I say about a father who drove the same blue van for 20 years and spent thousands of dollars to see my dream come true? What can I say about a sister and brother who, without jealousy, have always been there for me? What can I say to a family that never puts me on a pedestal, that sees my faults, my grumpy moods, my down days, and still loves me? What can I say? Saying "thank you" a million times would not be enough.

Born to humble beginnings with deformed feet, Kristi overcame all obstacles on the way to achieving her dream. She achieved it with a kind heart, a thoughtful and giving nature, and a love for whatever she set out to do. Kristi Yamaguchi is a real champion where it matters most, as a terrific role model and citizen not only for the Asian-American community, but for anyone who values genuine human qualities and a spirit that cannot be restrained from gliding gracefully and beautifully through life.

CHRONOLOGY

1971 Kristi Tsuya Yamaguchi is born on July 12 in Hayward, California. She has a foot deformity that requires orthopedic care.

1976 Young Kristi sees ice show at Southland Mall and is attracted to ice skating. She watches Dorothy Hamill win the Olympic gold medal at the 1976 Winter Olympics in Innsbruck, Austria. Hamill becomes Kristi's idol.

1977 Figure skating coach Ann Cofer begins training Kristi in skating basics.

1978 Kristi gives her first ice performance at the age of seven, coming in first place.

1980 She meets coach Christy Kjarsgaard, who becomes Kristi's full-time coach.

1982 At age 11, Kristi begins skating pairs with partner Rudy Galindo and coach Jim Hulick, while continuing to train for singles competitions.

1985 She leaves school and begins private tutoring on school subjects. She places fourth at U.S. Nationals in novice level singles; Yamaguchi and Galindo place fifth in junior pairs.

1988 Yamaguchi wins Worlds junior singles, and she and partner Rudy Galindo win Worlds junior pairs titles. She returns to school, attending Mission San Jose High for junior and senior years.

1989 Kristi is awarded silver medal at the U.S. Nationals; with Rudy Galindo she wins gold medal in Nationals pairs. She moves to Edmonton,

Alberta, Canada, 24 hours after graduating from high school to continue training with Kjarsgaard. Pairs coach Jim Hulick dies. Five days later, grandfather George Doi passes away.

1990   Yamaguchi defends U.S. Nationals pairs title, wins silver Nationals singles. After skating poorly at the Worlds, Yamaguchi decides to end pairs skating and focus on her singles training.

1991   She wins third U.S. Nationals silver medal and the Ladies Singles World Championships.

1992   She wins first U.S. Nationals title and Olympic gold medal, and repeats as Ladies Singles world

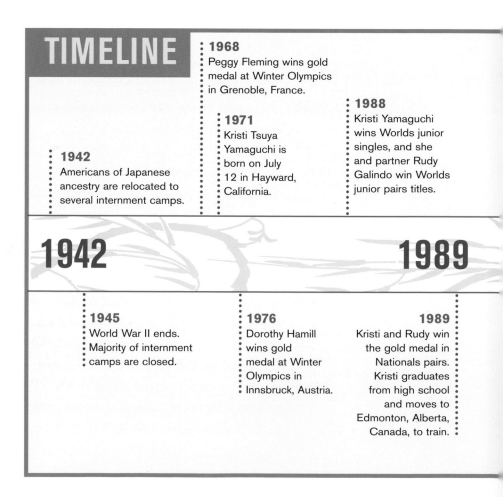

TIMELINE

1968
Peggy Fleming wins gold medal at Winter Olympics in Grenoble, France.

1971
Kristi Tsuya Yamaguchi is born on July 12 in Hayward, California.

1988
Kristi Yamaguchi wins Worlds junior singles, and she and partner Rudy Galindo win Worlds junior pairs titles.

1942
Americans of Japanese ancestry are relocated to several internment camps.

1942

1989

1945
World War II ends. Majority of internment camps are closed.

1976
Dorothy Hamill wins gold medal at Winter Olympics in Innsbruck, Austria.

1989
Kristi and Rudy win the gold medal in Nationals pairs. Kristi graduates from high school and moves to Edmonton, Alberta, Canada, to train.

champion. She wins her first World Pros Championship.

1993 Yamaguchi turns professional, signing on with *Stars on Ice.*

1994 She wins World Pros Championship and travels to Japan with goodwill delegation.

1996 Yamaguchi founds the Always Dream Foundation, a charitable organization. She wins World Pros Championship and U.S. Pro Championship, and is named Pro Skater of the Year.

1997 She co-authors book *Figure Skating for Dummies* with Kjarsgaard-Ness.

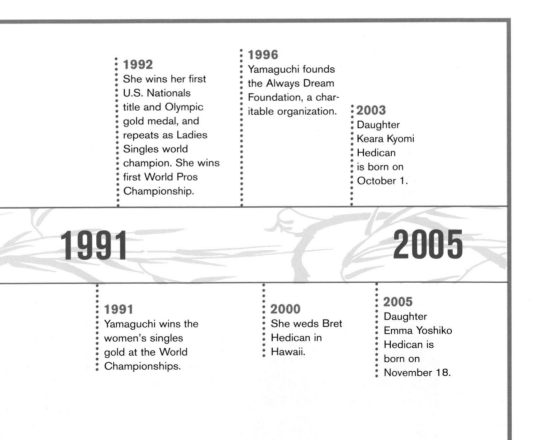

1992
She wins her first U.S. Nationals title and Olympic gold medal, and repeats as Ladies Singles world champion. She wins first World Pros Championship.

1996
Yamaguchi founds the Always Dream Foundation, a charitable organization.

2003
Daughter Keara Kyomi Hedican is born on October 1.

1991

2005

1991
Yamaguchi wins the women's singles gold at the World Championships.

2000
She weds Bret Hedican in Hawaii.

2005
Daughter Emma Yoshiko Hedican is born on November 18.

1998 Yamaguchi publishes her autobiography, *Always Dream*. She is inducted into the U.S. Figure Skating Hall of Fame.

1999 She is inducted into the World Figure Skating Hall of Fame.

2000 Yamaguchi and ice hockey pro Bret Hedican marry in Hawaii.

2002 Yamaguchi serves as Goodwill Ambassador for the Winter Games in Salt Lake City, Utah.

2003 She gives birth to a daughter, Keara Kyomi Hedican, on October 1.

2005 She gives birth to second daughter, Emma Yoshiko Hedican, on November 17.

2006 Yamaguchi is named host of figure skating reality series *Skating's Next Star*. Husband Bret Hedican and Carolina Hurricanes teammates win the NHL's championship, the Stanley Cup.

BIBLIOGRAPHY

Boedeker, Hal. "Another Skating Show Tosses Blades Into Ice Rink," *Orlando Sentinel* (March 20, 2006).

Donohue, Shiobhan. *Kristi Yamaguchi: Artist on Ice*. Minneapolis: Lerner Publications, 1994.

Jeansome, John. "Yamaguchi's Ancestors Are Japanese, but Figure Skating Star Is Just Your Typical California Kid." *Newsday* (February 2, 1992).

Kitano, Harry. *The Immigrant Experience: The Japanese Americans*. Philadelphia: Chelsea House, 1996.

Kule, Elaine. *Asian-American Biographies: Kristi Yamaguchi*. Chicago: Raintree, 2006.

Swift, E.M. "Ice Queens: Kristi Yamaguchi Led a U.S. Sweep at the World Figure Skating Championships." *Sports Illustrated*, Vol. 74, No.11 (March 25, 1991): p. 34(4).

———. "Next Stop, Albertville,"1992 U.S. Figure Skating Championships. *Sports Illustrated*, Vol. 76, No. 2 (Jan. 20, 1992): p. 32(3).

———. "Stirring: With Grace and Skill, Kristi Yamaguchi Skated Circles Around the Competition to Strike Gold." *Sports Illustrated*, Vol. 76, No. 6 (March 3, 1992).

Takai, Ronald. *Strangers From a Different Shore: A History of Asian Americans*. New York: Penguin Books, 1989.

Wellman, Sam. *Female Figure Skating Legends: Kristi Yamaguchi*. Philadelphia: Chelsea House, 1999.

Yamaguchi, Kristi, with Greg Brown. *Always Dream*. Dallas: Taylor, 1998.

WEB SITES

"About Japan." Inside Japan: Tours. Available online. URL: http://www.insidejapantours.com/about.shtml.

"Confinement and Ethnicity: An Overview of World War II Japanese American Relocation Sites." National Park Service: History. Available online. URL: http://www.cr.nps.gov/history/online_books/anthropology74/index.htm.

"Dorothy Hamill Bio." Academy of Achievement. Available online. URL: http://www.achievement.org/autodoc/page/ham1bio-1.

Official Website of the Olympic Movement. Available online. URL: http://www.olympic.org/.

International Skating Union. Available online. URL: http://www.isu.org/.

Japanese Culture. Available online. URL: http://www.japaneselifestyle.com.au/culture/culture.html.

Kids Web Japan. Available online. URL: http://web-japan.org/kidsweb/.

Kristi Yamaguchi's Always Dream Foundation. Available online. URL: http://www.alwaysdream.org/.

Official Kristi Yamaguchi Website. Available online. URL: http://rc.yahoo.com/promotions/kristi/index.html.

"Statue of Liberty." National Park Service. Available online. URL: http://www.nps.gov/stli/.

U.S. Figure Skating. Available online. URL: http://www.usfigureskating.org/.

FURTHER READING

Cooper, Michael. *Fighting for Honor: Japanese Americans and World War II*. New York: Clarion Books, 2000.

Grapes, Bryan. *Japanese American Internment Camps*. Chicago: Greenhaven Press, 2000.

Sinnott, Susan. *Extraordinary Asian Americans and Pacific Islanders*. New York: Children's Press, 2003.

Yamaguchi, Kristi, Jody Meacham, and Christy Kjarsgaard-Ness. *Figure Skating for Dummies*. New York: Hungry Minds, 1997.

PICTURE CREDITS

INDEX

ABOUT
THE AUTHOR

JUDY L. HASDAY, a native of Philadelphia, Pennsylvania, received her B.A. in communications and her Ed.M. in instructional technologies from Temple University. Hasday has written dozens of books for young adults, including the New York Public Library "Books for the Teen Age" award winners *James Earl Jones* (1999) and *The Holocaust* (2003), and the National Social Studies Council "2001 Notable Social Studies Trade Book for Young People" award winner *Extraordinary Women Athletes*. Her free time is devoted to volunteer work, photography, travel, and her pets.